ME, MYSELF, & I

ME, MYSELF, & I

DISCOVER YOURSELF WITH 50
REVEALING PERSONALITY QUIZZES

ROBERT ALLEN

BARNES & NOBLE BOOKS

NEW YORK

This edition published by Barnes & Noble, Inc., by
arrangement with Salamander Books Ltd.

2005 Barnes and Noble Books

M 10 9 8 7 6 5 4 3 2 1

ISBN 0-7607-6246-5

© Salamander Books, 2004

An imprint of Chrysalis Books Group plc

A CIP catalog record for this book is available from the
Library of Congress.

All correspondence concerning the contents of this book should
be addressed to Salamander Books.

CREDITS
Editor: Katherine Edelston
Designer: Cara Hamilton
Reproduction: Anorax Imaging Ltd.
Production: Alice Reeves

Printed in Malaysia

CONTENTS

HOW TO USE THIS BOOK

*H*umans are probably the world's most incurably curious creatures and the enigma of the human psyche is one of the subjects that has never ceased to fascinate us. If we were truthful with ourselves there is probably nothing many of us enjoy more than spending a couple of hours discussing our own thoughts and feelings with anyone who will listen.

There are many books available today that draw on our need to talk about ourselves and claim to provide us with instant self-analysis. In writing this book I have tried to approach the subject with a smile and a little humor. Most self-help books are usually interested in defining personalities in scientific terms, such as whether we are an introvert or extrovert, or if we possess a passive or aggressive character. This may be of great importance to psychologists but is this honestly what you want to know about yourself? My aim is to encourage you to think about how well you know your own nature. For example, how vain do think you are? Do you see yourself as grouchy or even-tempered? Do you think you possess that elusive element of *je ne sais quoi?* These might not be the kind of issues that excite your average psychologist but the answers to questions like these are often what we are most eager to understand about ourselves.

One of the greatest human virtues is our ability to laugh at ourselves. Where would we be without it? It is one of the things that make us strong and adaptable when life gets tough. So keep this in mind when reading this book and remember that not everything in it should be taken seriously. In fact, many of the questions I have included are there to make you smile or, with a bit of luck, laugh out loud.

There is only one thing left for me to say and that is simply to state that this book will not change your life. I do not claim to be able to help you to turn your life around but I do, however, hope that you will have some fun and discover a few new and interesting things about the way your mind works. You never know, you may well like what you find!

CHAPTER 1
THINK TANK

This first chapter will help you to determine how your thought processes work. Personality questionnaires tend to be fairly predictable so this chapter on the workings of the mind examines some slightly unusual, yet interesting, areas—subjects that are important aspects of our identity, and have great influence on our everyday lives, yet do not get the attention they deserve. Most of us like to think that we have some leadership potential but if we were faced with a situation that demanded us to take charge at a moment's notice, would we cope admirably or fall in quivering heap on the floor? Sometimes a great virtue is made of having an organized mind, but is it really such a wonderful gift or is it just an excuse for being unimaginative? Here, we look at these and other subjects such as ambition, optimism, and focus to probe the inner reaches of your psyche and find out what's going on in that head of yours!

Do you have a softer side?

Does your heart melt at low temperatures or is it made of stone? Are you just a pushover? Some of us cannot help being kind, considerate, and approachable while others are quite happy to kick kittens, shout abuse at children, and push little old ladies out of their way without a moment's hesitation. This test is designed to separate the good guys from the bad guys. Try and see just how you measure up.

1. **You are desperately trying to flag down a cab after a seriously long and stressful day at the office when you notice that nearby an elderly woman has dropped her groceries everywhere and is struggling to pick them up. Do you:**

A Miss five cabs while trying to chase down her canned goods. You are not that concerned about catching the the game tonight anyway and you would never forgive yourself if you just leave her there.

B Attract a friendly passer-by and tell them that you do not want to leave her but you will be late for an urgent appointment and you cannot possibly stop. This shows your desire to do the right thing while neatly passing the responsibility to someone else.

C Just grab a cab and go. She's not injured, you are tired, and it is definitely not worth missing the game to help her.

2. **You are in the backyard enjoying a cool drink in the midday sun when a frog hops past helplessly looking for water. Do you?**

A Take it to the nearest pond or lake and keep an eye on it to make sure that it does not stray again.

B Do the humane thing and take it to water just this once. Then leave it to its fate—you have better things to do.

C Just leave it. If the frog was stupid enough to go wandering around in the sun then it is not your problem.

3. **Your daughter comes home from school one day with a lost puppy which she says she wants to keep. Is your reaction to this request:**

A To proclaim that the puppy is the "cutest little thing you have ever seen" and welcome it into the family with open arms.

B Tell her, in a firm tone, that she will have to take it for walks and clean up after it, but you secretly think that the puppy is very cute.

C Tell her to put it back where she found it. If she wants a pet then how about something requiring less effort? Suggest a goldfish because it does not need walking.

4. **You go to see a romantic movie. During the final scene, the love-struck couple are finally reunited in a dramatic climax? How would you describe your reaction?**

A I am an emotional wreck as this unpredictable epic reaches a brilliant and happy ending. A masterpiece.

B I pretend not to be touched by the movie, but I know I will be rushing to rent it on DVD.

C I fell asleep half an hour ago and missed the final scenes. I only came to see the movie because my friend made me.

5. **What do you consider to be the best way to tell that special someone that you love them?**

A A torch song (you are allowed to assume you have song writing and singing ability).

B A really expensive gift. Nothing says "I love you" better than jewelry or, say, a subscription to digital TV.

C You do not need to do anything special as they know how you feel. Why spoil these tender feelings by expressing them outwardly?

6. **You married the love of your life fifteen years ago today. How do you celebrate this special day?**

A A surprise trip to one of the most beautiful and romantic cities in the world, preferably Paris, for the weekend. It will be a trip that you and your partner never forget.

B A romantic trip is far too expensive and will require more effort than you feel is truly necessary. You suggest going out for a nice meal at your favorite restaurant.

C You present them with a nice, moderately priced greeting card.

7. **You have been waiting at your favorite band's CD signing session and are told that you will be the last person to be seen by the band. The kid behind you bursts into tears at the news. Do you:**

A Sacrifice your place to let the kid meet the band. You know it is the right thing to do.

B You plead with the men on the door to let both of you in. Then it is their decision to turn down the crying child not yours.

C Just walk on in. You did not wait for hours to give in to some little kid's drama queen antics. It is probably just a stunt anyway.

8. You promised your son that if he got good grades at school you would take him to an amusement park, however he narrowly missed the grades. Do you:

A Take him to the park anyway. He tried hard which is all you can expect and you are not heartless.

B Agree to take him to the theme park but make it a condition that he works hard to improve his future grades.

C Send him to his room to study. Tell him the trip is off and explain the concept of "tough love."

9. You are a teacher marking test papers. You mark one student's paper and the total is just one point short of an A grade. Do you choose to:

A Re-mark the paper and find an excuse to give the additional point it needs to cross the threshold to greatness.

B Re-mark the paper just in case there was something you overlooked. The points you awarded are fair but not overly generous.

C Stick to the first result—it is the only reasonable way of marking the paper.

10. Do you approve of spending more than you can afford on your kids at Christmas?

A Yes, definitely. It gives you such a good feeling to see them happy, you cannot put a price on that kind of feeling.

B I spend money on my kids when I can but not necessarily all at Christmas. I need to think realistically about my finances as well.

C I can and do put a price on that kind of feeling and do not stretch a tight budget. Life is not about material goods anyway.

ANSWERS

An A scores 5 points, a B is worth 3, and a C is worth 2

45–50 The term "soft" does not really seem to do you justice, you are practically melting! You just need to make sure that your softer side does not make you a doormat for other people to walk all over. Just because you are a nice person at heart, it does not mean you have to sacrifice yourself or the things you love for others. This softness is commendable but sometimes you need to show a harder side. If, for example, you asked for certain grades and your child does not get them, what sort of model are you setting by showing that this failure does not really make any difference?

35–44 You like to make loving gestures and every now and again you make a really warm and heartfelt one that stands out. It seems that you are strong when you need to be, for example, marking the exam paper is a moral decision not one of a warm heart. If the answer is one mark off an A, then it should be given a B. You seem to know when to distinguish between occasions that call for a more formal approach than, say, taking your partner on a surprise holiday.

25–34 You are lacking the basis of a soft side although you are not completely immune to tender feelings. You should take care that your tendency to hard-heartedness does not push people away from you. For example, while you may love your partner, do they know that? How many inexpensive greeting cards will it take before they do not want to stick around anymore to find out?

Under 25 You are the hardest nut of them all! You have no softer side at all. You will have to learn when it is important to be formal and sincere, and learn when to let go and make a gesture. Either you cannot do this because you don't know how to, or because you do not want to. But if you cannot make the effort to try then you may well live to regret it.

Are you focused?

There are people whose concentration is like a laser beam. They can focus on one thing to the exclusion of anything else and they can keep it up for hours if necessary. The techicians who repair computer software, for example, are legendary for their ability to work day and night without letting their minds wander. Other people have minds like butterflies constantly alighting on one thought then another. No matter how hard they try, they end up being distracted by their surroundings. The purpose of this test is to help you decide which you are: laser beam or butterfly, or maybe you lie somewhere in between?

1. **You are reading a complicated book. Do you:**
A Keep having to re-read bits that you did not take in the first time.
B Read at a snail's pace and keep checking that you understand everything.
C You have the concentration of a brain surgeon. Nothing but *nothing* puts you off.

2. **You are on a long car journey. Do you:**
A Fall asleep after a short while. You can never remain awake in cars.

B Remember vaguely where you went but have no idea about the details of the route you took.
C You could describe the route for *National Geographic* if they would only pay you.

3. **A friend is talking to you while you prepare a meal. Would you:**
A Make encouraging noises while trying desperately to follow the recipe (and failing).
B Listen and cook at the same time but find it takes a lot longer than usual.

C Hold an indepth conversation about world politics while whipping together a perfect three course meal.

4. **Your boss insists on playing classical music in the office because he read somewhere that it helps concentration. Do you:**
A Become consumed by your hatred of classical music.
B Find it quite soothing but realize that you are spending too long listening

and not long enough working.
C You block it out. When you are working you are working—end of story.

5. **You stroll down to the local store and meet a neighbor on the way. Do you:**
A See him coming from a long way off. You were not really thinking about much anyway.
B See him just at the last minute and manage to say a quick hello without looking rude.
C Ignore him completely. You have a lot of important stuff to think about.

6. You are in a new town and stop to ask for directions. Do you:

A Get as far as, "Take a left by the Fire House," and forget all the rest.

B Remember the gist of the directions and, after a couple of mistakes, eventually find your destination.

C Fly like an arrow to the right place. You could still repeat what you were told the next day if you had to.

7. You attend a boring lecture. You would like to skip it but you are duty-bound to stay to the end. Would you:

A Gaze around the room, eat candy, and finally fall asleep.

B Struggle to stay awake and force yourself to take notes so that you can recall the important bits later.

C Find it easy to absorb the essential points even though you are bored by the lecture.

8. You have some work that must be completed to a deadline. Do you:

A Become distracted and call your client to beg for extra time.

B Become distracted at first but when the deadline approaches you are able stay focused long enough to get the job finished.

C You stay so fiercely focused that you finish the job early. You do not let the client know—they might expect you to lower your price!

9. With just a couple of days left to the holiday season you go Christmas shopping. Do you:

A Get bored, phone a friend, and end up having lunch together instead.

B Try frantically to get everything done but find that when you get home you have, as usual, forgotten several of the important presents.

C You tackle the task methodically using a computer-generated list that you update each year. It takes four hours but you get everything on your list with no omissions.

10. You are driving over a stretch of rough terrain in a 4x4. Do you:

A Constantly hit potholes and obstacles because you are too busy fiddling with the radio and checking your hair in the rearview mirror.

B Manage quite well so long as you can stop for frequent breaks to refresh yourself.

C You have the concentration and persistence of a rally driver. Nothing ever puts you off.

ANSWERS

Score 4 points for an A, 3 for a B, and 2 for a C

35–40 You focus only with great difficulty and only for short periods of time—goldfish have greater powers of concentration than you. This means that there are several career choices that you need to avoid—brain surgery and air traffic control spring to mind. To be honest there is nothing good about the inability to concentrate. It means that you are always forgetful and inefficient. However, there are exercises you can do to improve and you should consider finding yourself a course of treatment right now . . . before you forget!

30–34 You can concentrate when you have to. You are fairly focused as long as you do not have to keep it up for too long and you can relax occasionally. Most of the time you can be relied on not to wreck the car because you got distracted by something else. You could concentrate better if you really tried. All you need to do is make a determined effort to stick to whatever you are doing and refuse to be diverted. It will be tricky at first but you will get the hang of it eventually.

25–29 You are really very focused and you have no trouble at all staying with one thought or activity for as long as necessary. You are ideally suited to careers that demand a high level of concentration because you can be depended upon not to let your mind stray at vital moments. However, you are not so focused that you fail to pay attention to what goes on around you. You are not one of those people who are completely unapproachable while engaged on a task.

Under 25 You have a rare level of concentration. This is a very useful ability and you will be in great demand for certain tasks. You could be an excellent chess player and, assuming you had the inclination, surgery might also be a good choice. Your only problem is that you concentrate so intensely that sometimes you cut yourself off from the rest of the world for long periods. This can be irritating for those around you and, on occasion, it might be quite dangerous for you—simply crossing the road, for example, could prove hazardous!

HOW PERSISTENT ARE YOU?

Opposite is a very unusual maze. It was originally composed by the indefatigable Henry Dudeney. Most mazes have only one possible route from start to finish but this one has literally hundreds of correct routes and your task is to calculate just how many routes there are. As you will quickly find the pattern of the maze is such that it affects your vision quite badly. After staring at it for a few seconds you will start to experience odd visual distortions that make counting the routes especially difficult. There is a rumor that one puzzle fan became so obsessed with this maze that he drove himself to suicide. Do not do that. When you run out of new routes simply look up our answer on page 256. You may be surprised to find just how many there actually are.

Are you intuitive?

Some people claim that they know when the phone is about to ring, can detect an "atmosphere" in a building where dramatic events took place, or have a sense of foreboding when danger approaches. Others say that this is nonsense. Do your mental antennae twitch and warn you of events that are hidden from your regular senses or have you a down-to-earth approach, believing only in what you can see? Now is the time to find out.

1. **A FRIEND ARRIVES AT YOUR DOOR UNEXPECTEDLY. DO YOU:**

A Immediately sense that she has left her husband and come to you for support.

B Say, "Is there anything wrong?"

C Say, "I haven't seen you for ages. Where's Bill?"

2. **THE PHONE RINGS LATE AT NIGHT. DO YOU:**

A Rush to take the call. You just know that it is a relative with bad news.

B Answer and say, "Just what time do you think this is?"

C Turn over and go back to sleep. It is bound to be a wrong number.

3. **YOU GET AN UNEXPECTED LETTER. DO YOU:**

A Open it immediately because you are sure that it contains good news.

B Open it with some dread. You are not sure what is in it but you fear the worst.

C Leave it for later. It is probably just junk mail.

4. **YOUR BOSS ARRIVES UNEXPECTEDLY AT YOUR FRONT DOOR. HE NEVER NORMALLY CALLS ON YOU AT HOME. DO YOU:**

A Realize at once that he has come to tell you that your manager has had a serious accident and he wants you to take over.

B Assume, quite wrongly, that he has found out that you faked illness for two days last week.

C Say, "Hi, Bob, to what do I owe this pleasure?"

5. **YOU HAVE A DREAM IN WHICH YOU SEE YOURSELF INVOLVED IN A TRAFFIC ACCIDENT. DO YOU:**

A Take the bus to work the next day. Sure enough you learn later that there was a major accident on your usual route.

B Drive anyway but take extra care.

C Take no action at all. You never remember dreams anyway.

6. **WHEN PEOPLE TALK TO YOU DO YOU:**

A Read between the lines and extract hidden meaning from what they say.

B Take what they tell you at face value.

C Pay little attention. You are more interested in getting them to listen to you.

7. YOU GO TO SEE A PSYCHOLOGICAL THRILLER AT THE MOVIES. DO YOU:

A Guess in the first ten minutes of the movie exactly what is going to happen.

B Feel a sense of anticipation but only when it is obvious that something is about to happen.

C Fall asleep from boredom—you only went because your friends insisted.

8. YOUR CAT REGULARLY WALKS AROUND CERTAIN SPOTS IN YOUR HOUSE. DO YOU:

A Assume that the cat can see things you cannot, such as, ghosts.

B Assume that the cat is responding to perfectly natural sounds that are outside your hearing range.

C Who cares? It is just a dumb cat!

ANSWERS

Score 4 points for an A, 3 for a B, and 2 for a C

35–40 Your intuition is so highly developed that you could be psychic. Your antennae are constantly twitching as you receive ideas and sensations that are not immediately obvious to the rest of us. If you use your powers wisely you will be highly valued for the insights that you bring to other people. You should beware of using your intuition to give people information they are not capable of appreciating. Remember that others may be slower to understand these matters and you could cause them worry if you give them uncontrolled access to all that you know.

30–34 You have quite well-developed intuitive powers but these fall well short of ESP. You do, however, have a very useful ability to sense an "atmosphere" and you can "see" things that are not apparent to others. If you work on this you will be able to improve your intuitive powers. This is a very useful talent and it would be worth the effort—those with good intuition are valuable because they are often able to understand the undercurrents of a situation when others find it inexplicable.

9. SOMEONE SUGGESTS USING A OUIJA BOARD AT A PARTY. DO YOU:

A Enthusiastically agree. You have always wanted to take part in a séance.

B Agree with some reservations. You think people will probably just fake the whole thing.

C Laugh at such a silly suggestion. What a waste of time!

10. DO YOU SOMETIMES DISTRUST PEOPLE ON SIGHT?

A Yes, and I am usually right to do so.

B I try not to judge people until I know them better.

C Of course I distrust people, but it is nothing to do with intuition it is just that most people will try to get away with whatever they can.

25–29 You have no special intuitive talent. You have the ability within you but, because you do not really believe in it, it remains undeveloped. You have been brought up to appreciate and practice a "common sense" attitude to life and to avoid anything that smacks of the paranormal. When your sixth-sense attempts to tell you something you simply will not listen unless you can rationalize the information in some way. This is a great shame because it cuts you off from a whole area of life that is both interesting and rewarding.

Under 25 Put simply, there are rocks with more intuition than you! You must be the most unimaginative, closed-minded person. You cannot understand that it is possible to look at the world from a different angle, one that does not depend on logic and the normal five senses. As for having an "inner voice," you have no chance of finding it. What is really sad is that, as well as lacking intuition yourself, you probably also try to undermine the intuitive insights of others. This is a great shame because often they will have much to offer.

Are you an optimist?

Remember the story about the guy who fell off the Empire State Building? As he passed each floor on the way down people heard him saying, "So far so good. So far so good . . ." Is this you? Is your glass always half full and never half empty? Do you always walk on the sunny side of the street with a smile on your face? Or do you know that everything is going to go wrong and that, as life is looking good, disaster is bound to strike. Take this test to discover how optimistic you are.

1. You are in the car with your partner and screaming children driving to the airport to catch a plane to your vacation destination. The gas tank warning light came on ten minutes ago. Do you:

A Drive on regardless—it is not too far to the airport and luck is definitely on your side.

B Ask your partner what you should do and then drive on anyway. That way you can blame him when the plan goes wrong. Besides he is strong, he can walk and get some gas if necessary!

C Guess that you probably don't have enough fuel to get you to the airport, so you try to find the nearest gas station.

D Assume that you are going to run out of fuel and stop the car at the next available opportunity. You walk to the nearest gas station yourself, as your partner is bound to get lost.

2. You apply for a new job and are invited for an interview. When you arrive, you see that there are ten candidates for the position. How do you feel about this?

A These people are wasting their time applying for a job that is already yours. You are confident that there is no one better for the job than you.

B There appear to be some definite rivals for the job you want but you have good enough qualifications to be confident, even if you did get coffee on your suit on the way over.

C You immediately assume that the other candidates are better than you and, as a result, you underperform in the interview.

D These people are clearly superior. You are intimidated and leave knowing they will probably go for the guy wearing the nice (clean) suit.

3. You wanted to go to a concert but tickets have sold out. However, you discover that a radio station is giving a pair of tickets away in a competition. Do you:

A Enter confident that somebody has got to win the tickets and it is just as likely to be you as anybody else.

B Enter several times in an attempt to swing the odds in your favor.

C Enter once but then forget about it, expecting that you will not win anything.

D Do not even bother to enter—what chance have you really got of winning?

4. You have just finished spreading jelly over a slice of a toast. As you turn to walk over to the breakfast table you trip and the toast falls off the dish hurtling at great speed toward the ground. Finish the story:

A Suddenly the cupboard door swings open, and what should fall out but another dish for the toast to fall on to, jelly-side up.

B The toast lands on the floor, jelly-side up, so you dust it off and eat it anyway.

C The toast teeters on the verge of landing jelly side up, before falling the other way leaving you speechless.

D You do not even look. You simply go and make more.

5. After a long meeting you arrive home very late at night, hastily park the car in the drive, and go straight to bed. Just as you are about to drift off you realize that you have left one of the windows of your car open. Do you:

A Just leave it and go to sleep—you live in a nice safe neighborhood. Who would be malicious enough to break in to your sports car?

B Leave it, but set your alarm a bit earlier to go out and check on your car. It's not a great idea, but since you are tired, logic is not a priority.

C Get out of bed, go downstairs, close the window, and turn on the alarm. You can never be too careful.

D Assume that the car will have already been broken into by now, so you turn over and go to sleep. You will sort it out in the morning, if the car has not been stolen during the night.

6. You forget that you have to give a presentation on Monday morning. It is Sunday night, how do you respond to your error of judgement?

A Improvise! Use some of your trademark charm and charisma as well as some objects found around the house to make your presentation a success. How can you fail with finger puppets?
B Rise early and throw some ideas together before you have to leave.
C Stay up all night in a desperate attempt to squeeze a week's worth of work into just a few hours.
D Call and make your excuses blaming illness—you know the presentation will be a total disaster and it is not worth the humiliation.

7. Your kids have lost their eight month old kitten. It escaped through the front door and has not been seen since. What do you do?

A Assume that cats always come home eventually so you tell your kids that everything is going to be fine, Fluffy will wonder home in a couple of days.
B Start a campaign of posters to try and track it down.
C Attempt to replace the kitten with another one. You have no faith in your kids' ability to recognize their own pet.
D Don't bother looking for the cat. Tell your kids that Fluffy is never coming back—they need to learn the facts of life.

8. You want to go to the beach tomorrow but, though sunny today, the weather person says it will rain. How much notice do you take of this advice?

A None at all. You believe that they draw the weather forecast out of a hat, at random. You assume it is going to be sunny.
B You check other weather forecasts to try and get a broader picture, but probably end up going to the beach and hoping for the best.
C You plan to do something that is not beach-based to avoid the disappointment of sitting on the sand in the rain.
D You stay in. You are certain it will rain so what is the point?

9. You had arranged to go on a spring hiking vacation with friends. Several weeks beforehand you injure your ankle and the doctor tells you that you probably will not heal in time. Do you:

A Assume that you will be fine and book your accommodation anyway. After all you are a fast healer and doctors do not know everything.

B Wait until the last moment before having to make a decision but tell your friends to count on you.

C Tell your friends that you probably will not be coming, although you still hope that you will be better in time.

D Tell them outright that there is no way you will be able to come.

10. Your partner is the family cook. You are an expert at heating frozen ready-meals. You have a dinner party planned for tonight, but in the morning your partner is forced into an urgent meeting—so it is all up to you! What do you do?

A You attempt to cook the meal your partner was planning, following their recipe. You overcome your lack of cooking experience and the meal is a complete success.

B You attempt to follow the recipe. You recruit some help from a suitable source, a parent for example, and then pass the whole thing off as an individual effort.

C You warn all your friends in advance that the meal you have created is not up to your partner's standards. You point out that you deserve extra credit for even attempting it.

D You just cancel the whole thing telling your friends that you would like to cook but it is just bound to be a complete disaster.

ANSWERS

An A is worth 4 points, a B is 3, a C is 2, and a D is 1

35–40

You are walking a fine line between optimism and blind faith! While your unfaltering optimism must be commended, it never seems to be based upon much logic. Sometimes you seem to neglect important factors when you make these decisions. If you want to risk being stuck in a cramped car with no gas and screaming children in the back, then you are either very brave or stupid!

25–34

You are more of a realist. It is fair to say that a cupboard door opening and a new dish falling out is probably at the wrong end of the probability scale, but it is not too much to ask for the toast to land the right way up, is it? Your natural blend of optimism with a sense of logic is a good way to handle the problems of everyday life.

15–24

You are essentially a pessimist and, although you try to get on with life despite regular set backs, you do not believe in yourself and underperform as a result. If it is worth applying for a job despite the amount of competition for it, then it is surely worth making a credible effort. Your lack of faith in yourself and apparently in life as a whole sees you cruising through it without ever really trying hard, or believing in anything. Try to see the silver lining behind the clouds occasionally.

Below 15

You will eventually find yourself filled with regrets due to an incredible lack of ambition and motivation to do anything. Sure, you could have attempted to cook the meal your partner was planning for a dinner party, and it could have gone very, very wrong, but so what? Put it down to experience and try again. While you may think you are not risking anything if you take this pessimistic stance to your life, you will not gain anything either. In the end, it is the risks you take that define whether you win or lose.

Are you a natural leader?

Do you naturally take charge? When there is an emergency are you the one who steps in to save the day? When something needs organizing are you the one who establishes a team and gets the job done? If so, you may be a natural leader. Our society values leadership skills very highly and many people try to convince themselves and others that they possess them. However, the truth is that most of us are not natural leaders and this is not a bad thing—where would the leaders be if they did not have a followers to order around? To see where you stand take a few minutes to answer these questions.

1

After struggling back from the local hardware store with a flatpack table requiring "some self-assembly" you and your family eventually get it home and attempt to put it together. Do you:

A Locate the instruction manual and then stand back and orchestrate the whole operation without actually putting anything together yourself.

B Become proactive and lead the way by starting to put parts of the table together yourself, while also telling others what to do.

C Wait until another family member gives you something to do, but do not actually try and do anything yourself—instruction manuals are tricky things.

D Offer to make some coffee for all those involved so you can stay out of the whole table-building exercise.

2

You go to a restaurant with friends, and after the usual menu reading a waitress comes to the table to take your order. Do you:

A Take control of all the ordering. You also choose the wine and then, when it arrives, you are the one to taste it. If people have not finished deciding what they want yet, you help them decide!

B Ask your friends if they have finished deciding what they want to eat, and if they have not, ask the waitress to give you a few more minutes.

C When the waitress asks you if are ready to order, try to pass the responsibility to somebody else.

D Look away and try not to make eye contact! If you pretend you have not seen the waitress then she will have to ask somebody else.

3

You go to the movie theatre with a new love interest. You cannot decide what movie you want to see and when you ask their opinion, they say they have no preference. Do you:

A Confidently choose a movie without checking what it is about. You trust your instincts and are sure to make a good choice.

B Wait until you get to the cinema and find details of the movies showing. You are assertive and pick one, but check with your partner before buying any tickets.

C Say that you are not bothered either way and just choose a movie at random from the list when you reach the cinema.

D Avoid a potentially awkward situation by telling your partner you have to go to the restroom. Leave them to make the decision while you are away.

4

Visiting an amusement park, you remember that your friend does not like rollercoasters. You do. You even have a key ring containing a picture of you falling down a hundred foot drop on another rollercoaster. How do you cope with this difference of interests?

A Tell your friend that this hundred foot drop is completely different from the one that made your friend violently sick last time. A little white lie never hurt anyone.

B Try to convince your friend that they should at least try one of these rides or they will regret it later. If they still hate them afterwards then you will never ask them to try again.

C Ride the kids' carousel all day while bottling up your anger, knowing that you would rather be hurtling around a metal track at great speed acquiring a bad case of motion sickness.

D Spend the majority of time in one of the many bars and restaurants in the café areas and carefully avoid going on anything too controversial.

5

You overhear some close friends of a work colleague talking about plans for their birthday. They were thinking of organizing a party but nobody has bothered to put any effort into doing so. Now it seems that nothing is going to happen. Do you:

A Organize the party yourself! You do not really know them that well but it is this kind of warm-hearted gesture that will make you friends. You could tell their friends, but why bother? They will only ruin it for you anyway.

B Suggest proposals for a party to their friends and try and get them to help out putting it all together. They are a close group but they need some help and encouragement.

C Suggest some ideas to one of their friends and try and get them to organize something but do not actually get involved with anything yourself—it is not your responsibility after all.

D Just pretend you did not hear anything and do not get involved. It is not your job to organize it and someone will have better ideas than you anyway.

6

Your sports team are head of the league and have an important game coming up. However, two hours before the vital game your coach becomes ill and is unable to decide on tactics and team selection. Do you:

A Remove the current captain of the team and make yourself the replacement. Then tell the other team members the tactics for the upcoming game. You will lead your team to a glorious victory!

B Let the captain take charge of the team in the absence of a coach but make suggestions on tactics and team selection.

C Just sit back and let everyone else worry about it. You do not want to risk using your tactics and then losing the game. You just do what you are told.

D Let one of the second team players convince you that they should have your place in the team—they probably know best anyway.

7

You and some friends are given the task of constructing a mural to be hung in the children's unit of the local hospital. You all have ideas of your own. Do your friends:

A Immediately come to you with different ideas and ask you to pick the one you like best. Naturally they give you the deciding vote.

B All pick someone else's idea but still have strong reservations and you tell them you are not that keen on it. Eventually they go with the one you wanted even though they do not like it as much.

C Ask you your opinion on which idea you think would be best, but if your idea does not correspond with theirs then they discard your opinion.

D Not bother asking your opinion.

8

As part of a teambuilding exercise six blindfolded people must erect a tent. You, however, can see and must give them instructions. How would you respond to this challenge?

A Work out the various small jobs that need to be done and decipher the order in which these jobs have to be completed. Then choose members of the group with the right strengths to complete each section.

B Try to do the whole thing on your own, you make a bit of a mess of it and the tent ends up being constructed so poorly that a small gust of wind could knock it down.

C Get someone else to help you instruct the team. You cannot see round both sides of the tent anyway, and you cannot even put a tent up yourself let alone instruct someone else to!

D Get a blindfold and ask to become a helper—let somebody else worry about instructing.

9

You are the captain of sinking cruise liner. How would you deal with hundreds of terrified screaming passengers as well as your own fear?

A I would estimate how many lifeboats there are and the number of passengers in order to find the best way to get everyone off the ship. Then I would prioritize people in terms of lifeboats, calm everyone down, and find the quickest and most effective way to get people out.

B I would try to help passengers get off the liner as best I could but because of the scale of the job I would enlist help from others. I cannot be expected to evacuate an entire cruise ship on my own after all!

C I would not even bother trying to be a leader, this sort of thing was not mentioned in the training! I would put my first mate in charge and tell him it is his day to shine. Then I would go and find a lifeboat.

D I would take refuge inside the ship and hope the whole thing blows over, fingers crossed.

10

You are a teacher taking a group of young kids on a field trip to a museum. The kids are running wild. Are you capable of taking control?

A Yes, you instantly regain control and take them on an enriching adventure through world history.

B The majority of the kids respect you, and are responsive when you call for their attention, however a couple of the more troublesome ones pay little notice of you and continue running around the museum causing trouble.

C Only the star pupils seem to listen while everyone else pays no attention whatsoever and continue to cause mayhem. You eventually get a fellow teacher to calm things down for you.

D Nobody listens, including the other teachers who just do not seem to care. You and your class are ejected from the museum.

ANSWERS

Mostly As You are a strong and effective leader. However, while other people around you may respect you, do they really like you? You need to be considerate of other ideas and opinions so people feel that they can relate to you. This is also a crucial factor in making others look up to you.

Mostly Bs You seem hell bent on wanting to lead but sometimes this faith in your own ability is misguided and you do a bad job as a result of your insistence on leading without the help of others. There is no shame in getting some things wrong, but it is wrong to struggle on without asking for help.

Mostly Cs You show signs of wanting to lead, but lack the confidence and often ask for help when you don't really need it. You should trust your instincts more and believe in your ability to gain respect from others, and your ideas will be well received.

Mostly Ds People are not valuing you or your work highly enough. Your inability to put yourself and your views in the open will undoubtedly leave you unfulfilled and with regrets. If you cannot be a leader, then at least make sure that you are listened to and respected by the person who is.

Do you have an organized mind?

Are you a neat, tidy, alphabetically-ordered sort of person? Or is your life located deep in the suburbs of Slobville? Can you easily find things you need because "everything has its own place," or do you have to spends hours rummaging through mountains of clutter on the floor? Is it easy for you to find a clean shirt? Some people are so neat that they drive you crazy with a mixture of frustration and envy. You wonder how they manage to look as though they were, until recently, packed in cellophane. At the opposite end of the organizational spectrum are those who look permanently crumpled, and seem to be completely incapable of arranging their lives. This test sorts the ultra-neat from the desperately disheveled.

1. IN YOUR OPINION THE POINT OF CUSHIONS ARE TO:

A Provide color coordination and symmetry for your furniture.
B Make the couch look good and more comfortable.
C Hide the red chili stain on the couch that you do not want you partner to see.

2. IN YOUR OPINION FENG SHUI IS?

A A fantastic method by which you are able to free your living space of clutter and mess and create an environment of freedom and spaciousness.
B A completely misinterpreted and misunderstood Chinese art that does not solve any tidiness issues.
C A load of garbage.

3. **IN YOUR OPINION WHAT WOULD A WORLD WITHOUT COASTERS BE LIKE?**

A Not worth living in! There would be marks on everything, nobody would know where to put their drinks! Inevitably complete anarchy would come as a result.

B Very similar to the existing one. We could kill two birds with one stone and discard place mats as well.

C I would need to have owned some coasters in order to answer this question. I have just been sitting my cups on top of the presentation I have been doing for work these last six months.

4. **THE PROSPECT OF WEARING AN UNIRONED SHIRT:**

A Is an unthinkable one. I would rather be late or even not go into work rather than wear an unironed shirt. Appearance is everything and looking untidy would certainly affect my work.

B An unfortunate one but when you oversleep you just have to live with it. I will try and cover it up by wearing a jacket over the top and nobody need ever know.

C An almost everyday occurrence and by doing it so often I have lowered people's expectations of me.

5. **YOU ARE ASKED TO BE THE BEST MAN AT YOUR FRIEND'S WEDDING. WITH SO MUCH TO DO AND SO MUCH TO ORGANIZE HOW DO YOU HANDLE THIS RESPONSIBILITY?**

A You barely even stop to take a breath as you phone caterers, florists, and everyone else in a cool methodic way and everything goes as planned. You even remember the rings, and the ceremony and reception are a success.

B You try to do a thorough job but inevitably forget something at the last minute causing widespread panic. However, the job has been well-executed considering you were half asleep when you were asked to do it, as you have been most of the way through the project.

C You forget you are the best man until two days before the wedding and end up asking friends to help you save the situation. Even so you do a very poor job.

6. **AFTER A DINNER PARTY IT'S LATE, YOU ARE TIRED AND IN NEED OF SLEEP. CAN THE DIRTY CROCKERY WAIT UNTIL THE MORNING?**

A No, you will simply lie in bed thinking about the dishes that await you in the morning. There is something satisfying and secure about knowing the house is in perfect order.

B You start washing up but give up half way through—you are too sleepy and you are not washing them correctly. Go to bed now—it will all still be waiting there for you in the morning.

C Go to bed without even thinking about washing the dishes. You are not even sure if you will clean them tomorrow.

7. **WHAT IS YOUR OPINION OF PEOPLE WHO STORE THEIR CDS ALPHABETICALLY AND THEIR MOVIES BY COLOR CODED SYSTEMS CLASSIFIED BY DIFFERENT GENRES?**

A It is the only way of ensuring quick and easy access to all your favorite movies and music—how else would you possibly find anything?

B I make an attempt to put my CDs into some kind of order. But, to be completely honest, I would rather spend my time listening to my music than organizing it.

C Most of my CDs do not have boxes, or are in the wrong boxes, or the boxes do not have CDs in them—so any kind of organization is going to prove difficult. Besides I would never stick to it anyway.

8. IS IT ACCEPTABLE TO WEAR COLORS THAT DO NOT MATCH EVEN WHEN YOU ARE JUST HANGING AROUND THE HOUSE WATCHING TV?

A No, just because there is nobody else around is no excuse. You have a duty to yourself to look good and putting red with green is something that should not be done unless it is Christmas.

B If there is a chance someone might come over then you make sure you look reasonably presentable but, for you, comfort will always come before looking good when you are relaxing.

C Just hanging around the house? I will be wearing these clothes to work tomorrow!

9. MY HOUSEHOLD TRASH IS:

A Carefully divided into plastics, newpapers, and glass to make recycling easier. I enjoy sorting everything out.

B More or less where it should be. Everything is in its correct place except last night's trash which I left in the yard because I was too tired to make it to the garbage.

C A large pile of unsorted waste that I will at some point have the unenviable task of having to sort out into separate piles, but I'm not sure when that will happen.

10. I SEE A BAD HAIR DAY AS:

A A styling challenge that I will eventually overcome and conquer leaving for work with brilliant hair defying all the odds!

B One of those things that cannot be avoided I try not to let it affect my work or my confidence and just assume that tomorrow will be better.

C More or less the same as every other day. I put the same minimal effort into my hair as usual. I call it my rugged look.

ANSWERS

Score 4 points for every A, 3 for a B, and 2 for a C

35–40 You have really got everything planned. Congratulations! You would make an excellent wedding planner. However, you need to try and stop worrying so much about the superficial side of life, especially in situations where you have nobody to impress but yourself. While you are seen as reliable, is this what you want? Are you really content with who you are, always concerned about minor unimportant details such as hairstyles and cushions?

30–34 Clearly you are tidy but not obsessive about it. In the same way you are organized but also know how to have a good time when such an opportunity arises. In this way you are able to portray an image of yourself that is both reliable and fun-loving and because of this you are a good friend. Perhaps on occasions you are still trying too hard to impress, even though you are content with being a slob when you are on your own!

25–29 We are in slob territory now! You need to get some order in your life or people will stop respecting you. It is wrong to suggest that people judge you only on appearance, but in terms of first impressions, if you really want people around you to take what you have to say seriously, then you need to put some effort in. If you do not, people will just stop listening and you will end up losing out. Occasionally you do come through for people but your tendency to be unreliable is causing you to lose friends.

Under 25 Your road to recovery starts here because you are underachieving. More to the point you are just making things more difficult for yourself. You have to recycle so why turn it into one long never ending job when it does not have to be. Short-term laziness is going to cause you long-term problems if you cannot find a way of getting some order into your life.

WHAT IS THE LINK?

Psychologists believe that there is a strong correlation
between intelligence and the ability to handle words. Basically,
the quicker you solve the puzzle opposite the brighter you
are. At first sight the listed words have nothing to do with
each other. If, however, you look at them carefully you will
discover a connection. What could it be? You only need to
spot something interesting about one of them and the others
will quickly fall into place. The answer
is on page 256 but no cheating!

EVENTS

LINE

NAILED

WANDER

EEL

SAILS

RICE

LYRIC

How angry do you get?

We can all become a little aggravated now and again. Life is full of frustrations and there never seems to be a lack of events that irritate us. But do you take it all philosophically and get on with your life or are you angry and shouting before you realize that you're upset? Try this test and find out whether you are a laid back dude or a volcano waiting to erupt.

1. YOU ARE LATE FOR A MEETING BUT THE CAR IN FRONT OF YOU IS BEING DRIVEN BY AN OLD LADY DOING 20MPH. THERE IS NO WAY TO GET PAST HER SAFELY. DO YOU:

A Take a deep breath and wait patiently for her to turn off. After all, we will all be old one day.

B Flash your lights, honk the horn, and wave like a maniac at her to move over and let you pass.

C Use your cell phone to call the police. You report a bank robbery and give them a description of the old lady's vehicle as the getaway car.

2. YOU TAKE YOUR FAMILY OUT FOR A MEAL. THE WAITRESS IS HOPELESS. SHE NOT ONLY MIXES UP YOUR ORDER BUT MAKES IT QUITE CLEAR SHE COULD NOT CARE LESS. DO YOU:

A Say nothing. When you get home you write a strong letter of complaint to their head office.

B Call the manager over and complain about the poor quality of service.

C Say loudly to the waitress, "I'm sorry to have inconvenienced you, I mistook this place for a restaurant!" Then demand a full refund.

3. YOUR BOSS KEEPS PICKING ON YOU FOR SILLY LITTLE FAULTS THAT HE OVERLOOKS IN YOUR CO-WORKERS. DO YOU:

A Say nothing and make a big effort to improve your performance.

B Sue the company on the grounds that you are being bullied.

C Phone your boss's wife and tell her about the intimate late nights that he has been having with his secretary.

4. YOU HAVE BEEN PULLED OVER BY A COP BECAUSE YOU WERE DRIVING SLIGHTLY OVER THE SPEED LIMIT. DO YOU:

A Apologize and accept the citation without any argument.

B Make a note of the officer's number and threaten to make an official complaint.

C Shout and scream. Tell him that the Chief of Police is a personal friend of yours and that he had better wave goodbye to his career.

5. YOU HAVE SPENT HOURS AT THE GROCERY STORE. YOU ARE TIRED AND WANT TO GET HOME AS QUICKLY AS POSSIBLE. AS YOU ARRIVE AT THE CHECKOUT SOMEONE PUSHES IN FRONT OF YOU. DO YOU:

A Ignore him. He is obviously too ignorant to have good manners.

B Tap him on the shoulder and tell him just how rude and thoughtless you think he is. (It's OK to do this as he is smaller than you.)

C Follow him to the parking lot and while he is busy loading the car you let the air out of his tires.

6. YOUR SON COMES HOME FROM SCHOOL WITH A TERRIBLE REPORT CARD. DO YOU:

A Explain the need for hard work and point out that people who don't study when they are young will only qualify for menial jobs when they finish school.

B Yell a lot and then ground him for a couple of weeks.

C Decide that the school is too laid back. Send him to military school.

7. YOU TAKE YOUR CAR TO BE SERVICED. WHEN YOU GET IT BACK IT'S CLEAR THAT SEVERAL IMPORTANT JOBS HAVE NOT BEEN DONE PROPERLY. DO YOU:

A Decide never to use that garage again.

B Phone the manager and demand that he repair all the faults.

C Park your car outside the garage bearing a large placard denouncing the company as a bunch of incompetents.

8. YOU ARE AT A FOOTBALL GAME AND YOUR TEAM GETS SLAUGHTERED. DO YOU:

A Have a beer and forget about it. Every team has its bad days.

B Shout abuse at everyone including the team, the coach, and the referee. What is wrong with these people?

C Take out an ad in your local paper announcing that you are switching your allegiance to another team who might actually have a chance of winning occasionally.

9. YOUR NEIGHBOR'S KIDS PLAY LOUD ROCK MUSIC AT ALL HOURS OF THE DAY AND NIGHT. DO YOU:

A Take no notice. After all, we were all kids once.

B Phone your neighbor and threaten legal action unless they stop the noise.

C Dig up the cable to their house and cut off their electricity.

10. YOUR FIRM GOES BUST AND YOU LOSE YOUR JOB. DO YOU:

A Move on and start looking for a new job.

B Tell the boss angrily that it is his incompetence that has caused the problem.

C Load your computer, and any other equipment you can get hold of, into your car before you leave. These people owe you big time and you are going to get what you can out of them.

ANSWERS

MOSTLY A'S

You are too reasonable for your own good. Being calm is an excellent thing but you have to be careful that people do not take advantage of your quiet nature and walk all over you. A little anger now and again can be therapeutic and you should really give it a try. At the moment you look like the guy who gets sand kicked in his face at the beach. Is that really what you want?

MOSTLY B'S

You do get the balance between being calm or angry right most of the time. You can be assertive when the situation demands and you know the best way to deal with others who are making your life difficult. Occasionally you get really angry but then so do most people. Your moderate approach is the right one. People know that there is a point beyond which it is dangerous to push you and they are careful not to reach that point. On the other hand, they also know that you will be calm and reasonable as long as they play the game.

MOSTLY C'S

Down tiger! This is everyday life. It is not supposed to be a warm-up for World War III. Try to chill a little or you will end up spontaneously combusting through sheer rage. It is OK to get angry sometimes but you approach life with a permanently hostile attitude. If you always look like you want a fight you are bound to find people who are ready to oblige. Do you really want to spend so much of your life involved in senseless conflicts? If the answer to that question is "Yes," then perhaps you need a course in anger management.

How honest are you?

We like to think we are all upright citizens but is it really true? Those pens on your desk, did you buy them or did they actually come from your office? Remember the other day when someone gave you too much change in a store? You didn't stop to point out the mistake did you? So what else would you be willing to do that is not quite honest? Is it really true that virtue is just a case of insufficient temptation? Use this test to discover the truth.

1

You are at an ATM and it gives you twice as much money as you asked for. Would you:
A Wait until the bank is open and go in to explain the mistake and give back the extra cash.
B Keep the money and say nothing.
C Try it again. Who knows, you might get even luckier the second time.

2

You find a wallet in the street containing a large sum of money, some credit cards, and a driver's license. Do you:
A Contact the owner and give the wallet back.
B Send back the credit cards and license anonymously but keep the money as your reward.
C Keep everything including the wallet. You go on a little spending spree with the credit cards.

3

A friend shows you a way to cheat on your expenses at work. The chances of being caught are negligible and you could make yourself an extra $500 per month. Would you:

A Refuse to have anything to do with it.

B Make a few extra bucks but soon give up because you are afraid of getting caught.

C Go for it! What kind of sap doesn't want to make some easy money? The company has always underpaid you anyway.

4

You get a big tax rebate that you are sure is a mistake. Would you:

A Phone the IRS and explain their mistake.

B Put the money to one side and wait to see if they notice the error.

C Spend the cash on something you have always wanted. The IRS has been stealing your money for years.

5

You get details of an internet con. Each person conned loses only a few dollars but you stand to make a huge amount of money. Would you:

A Have nothing to do with it and report the scam to the police.

B Try it just out of curiosity but stop before you get too involved.

C Work the con for all it's worth. Who are you really hurting anyway?

6

You do some voluntary work for a charity. Someone leaves a bequest but when the check arrives it has been made out to you personally. Do you:

A Redirect the money to the charity it was intended for.

B Agonize for days over what to do. Eventually you pay the money into the charity because you are afraid of being found out.

C Finders keepers! That check had your name on it so the money must have been meant for you, right?

7

Your water main breaks and your house is flooded. If the pipe has broken due to old age the insurance will not pay out. It would be quite easy to make it look like an accident so that you get paid. Would you:

A Tell the insurance company the true story.

B Try to make the broken pipe look like an accident but stop short of telling any actual lies.

C Fake an accident and brazen it out even when the insurers become suspicious about it.

8

You accidentally hit another car in a parking lot but no one saw you do it. Would you:

A Leave a note on the damaged car's windshield explaining what happened and your contact details.

B Leave a note of apology but no contact details.

C Drive away before anyone has a chance to spot you.

9

You find a counterfeit $50 bill in your wallet. It is a convincing fake that most people would not notice. Would you:

A Take it to the bank and tell them you think the bill is a phony.

B Keep the bill but wrestle with your conscience about whether you should pass it on to someone else.

C Find some sap to take the fake note off your hands.

10

You find a suitcase containing thousands of dollars in used bills of small denomination. There is no sign of ownership in the suitcase. Would you:

A Leave it where you found it. You've seen all those movies about people finding mob money.

B Take some of the money and leave the rest. Even if the cash is found no one will notice that you have dipped into it.

C You will never get a chance like this again so you take the whole lot. You use it to set up in a new location with a fake identity—say "hello" to the high life!

ANSWERS

Give yourself 1 point for an A, 2 for a B, and 3 for a C

Under 25 You are so honest that it is hard to believe that you are telling the whole truth. Can you honestly claim that you have never stolen a pen from the office? Or "forgotten" to pay your ticket on the train? Really? If that's true you must be a rare person. On the other hand, if you were trying to fool yourself it would be interesting to know why. Did you have a very strict upbringing? It seems that there is more to your obsessive honesty than meets the eye.

25–29 You are reasonably honest but are not averse to the odd moment of dishonesty if you think you won't get caught. You would not contemplate doing anything really dishonest (like defrauding a bank, for example), but you would certainly take advantage of any situation where you could make a little profit. You probably don't tell the whole truth on your tax returns and you probably cheat on your expenses at work. Be careful! It always looks easy but you would be surprised how often people like you get caught and are shocked to discover that others do not consider your offenses as minor as you do.

30–34 You really like to sail close to the wind, don't you? You are not nearly honest enough to stay out of trouble. You have a "finders keepers" attitude about everything that you come across. You have great difficulty understanding that certain behavior that you view as quite normal, is regarded as criminal by society as a whole. You badly need to reassess your attitudes before they get you into some real trouble.

35–40 You are probably reading this in your jail cell. You have no moral qualms at all when it comes to issues of honesty. You have never understood that it is wrong to help yourself to things that belong to other people. In spite of the fact that you have been caught and punished for your dishonesty you still do not understand that you need to change your ways. What a waste of your life!

How vain are you?

Most of us take an interest in how we look but, for some people, it becomes an obsession. Looking good, especially as we get older, takes time, money, and a lot of effort. Are you one of those people who thinks that nothing is more important than looking good or are you relaxed about your appearance?

1. **SOMEONE RINGS YOUR DOORBELL. DO YOU CHECK YOURSELF IN THE MIRROR ON THE WAY TO OPENING THE DOOR?**

A Of course not. It's probably only the mailman.

B Yes, I would take a quick peek to make sure my hair was not a mess.

C I usually send another member of the family. I do not like meeting strangers unless I have had a chance to spruce myself up properly beforehand.

2. **YOU REMEMBER HOW NARCISSUS FELL IN LOVE WITH HIS OWN REFLECTION. DOES THAT SOUND A BIT LIKE YOU?**

A Certainly not. As long as I am clean and tidy I don't care how I look.

B I like to look good but I am certainly not obsessed with my appearance.

C When you look this good a mirror is hard to pass up. Unless you keep checking there is always the chance that you might have a hair out of place.

3. DO YOU SPEND A LOT OF TIME COMPARING YOUR LOOKS WITH THOSE OF FRIENDS AND CO-WORKERS?

A Not at all. I think that is a very stupid and shallow way to behave.

B I must admit I keep an eye on the competition. You cannot let yourself get left behind can you?

C Keeping an eye on how other people look is vital. It is the only way to make sure you are ahead of the game. I need to know about new fashions before anyone else.

4. DO YOU SPEND MUCH ON BEAUTY PRODUCTS?

A Hardly anything. I buy value brands of soap and shampoo.

B I sometimes splash out on something to make me feel better but I do not let such spending get out of hand.

C Beauty products are essential to my way of life. Of course I spend a lot on them. To me putting on the right face cream is like a form of yoga.

5. WOULD YOU EVER CONSIDER PLASTIC SURGERY?

A No, I do not approve of interfering with nature like that.

B I might try it when I'm older. I'd like to fix the bits that start to sag.

C You are joking, right? I have been having nips and tucks since I was twenty.

6. **APART FROM HEALTH CONSIDERATIONS, WOULD YOU DIET JUST TO LOOK BETTER?**

A I think that dieting is silly and dangerous for people with no medical need to lose weight.

B I diet sometimes to make myself look better. I always feel it is a good idea to lose some weight in the summer before you hit the beach.

C I have been on a diet since I was sixteen. My latest involves a plate of raw liver each day. How can you keep looking good if you eat what you want?

7. **ON A SCALE ON 1–10 JUST HOW GORGEOUS ARE YOU?**

A What a ridiculous question! I would not dream of answering that.

B On a good day I guess I would give myself a 7 or an 8.

C 1–10 just does not give me enough scope. I am worth at least a 15.

8. **DO YOU EXPECT PEOPLE TO COMPLIMENT YOU ON YOUR APPEARANCE?**

A Of course not, and I would be very embarrassed if anyone did.

B It is nice to be noticed sometimes but I do not expect compliments all the time.

C You would better believe it. Anyone who doesn't compliment me is obviously visually impaired.

9. ARE LOOKS MORE IMPORTANT THAN PERSONALITY?

A Personality is obviously more important. You just have to look at Mother Theresa for an example.

B I think personality is important but, of course, I care what people look like as well.

C Who the heck is Mother Theresa? Anyone who doesn't look like a million bucks is just not on my planet.

10. YOUR PARTNER IS INVOLVED IN AN ACCIDENT THAT LEAVES THEM WITH A BAD FACIAL SCAR. WHAT WOULD YOU DO?

A My love does not depend on appearances. Anyway my partner would need my help in overcoming this terrible trauma.

B I'm not saying it would not be difficult for me to come to terms with this but I hope I would have the strength of character to do it.

C I am out of here! How could I be seen with anyone who was less than absolutely perfect?

ANSWERS

MOSTLY AS

You're not vain at all. You are very worthy and full of good character but no one will ever love you for your looks. You might try taking a little more interest in your appearance. It isn't a bad thing to want to look good for yourself. Your insistence that good looks don't matter sounds a little obsessive. What is it you are afraid of? Do you think you cannot compete and therefore you make out that you don't care? That's an old psychological trick but it isn't a good idea. You are cutting yourself off from a whole area of quite harmless enjoyment.

MOSTLY BS

You are not immune to vanity sometimes but you are no worse than most people. While enjoying looking good you should try not to lose sight of what really matters. Your attitude is balanced and mature. You know that looking good isn't the most important thing in the world but you don't reject it as being trivial either. You can take an interest in your looks when you want to, but you could easily ignore them when there are more important things to think about.

MOSTLY CS

As long as you breathe you will never lack someone to love you! You're so vain that you probably think this test is about you. Believe it or not there are other things in this world apart from you and a mirror. Maybe you should take some time away from yourself and try to find out what is really important in life. You probably think that only dull, boring people are not obsessed by their appearance but you are quite wrong. Your attitude is immature and shallow and, in the long run, will bring you no lasting happiness.

Are you ambitious?

Do you constantly plot and plan your rise up the corporate ladder? Is your whole life geared to achieving career goals? Do you live to work or work to live? This test is designed to see whether you spend every waking minute pursuing your ambitions or whether you are one of those contented souls who fill their lives with all sorts of activities that have nothing to do with work. This is the place to find out whether you are a corporate high-flyer in the making or whether you would rather leave the ambition to others while you play ball with your kids.

1. Where do you see yourself being in five years' time?

A I will be in senior management by then. With a bit of luck I might even be a company director.
B I will certainly have had a major promotion in that time.
C I would be expecting to be promoted by then.
D I never think that far ahead.

2. Do you have an eye on your boss's job?

A Of course, doesn't everyone? When the time is right I will make my move.
B I have thought about it a lot. The competition would be very stiff.
C I don't really like the idea of so much responsibility.
D I would hate to do all the things she/he does. She/he has no life.

3. **How much money do you want to earn?**

    A You should always earn more than double your age. For example, at twenty-five you should be earning over $50,000.
    B I need a high salary because I enjoy quite a high maintenance lifestyle.
    C I like to have money but I don't need to be rich.
    D There are so many things more important than money.

4. **Do you ever doubt that your ability could take you to the top?**

    A Not for one second. If you think that way you will never make it.
    B I try not to have doubts but it isn't always easy.
    C I often have doubts but struggle hard to overcome them.
    D I don't think I would ever reach the top because I don't really want to.

5. **Do you see co-workers as friends or rivals?**

    A They're rivals, of course! You can't trust co-workers as far as you can spit.
    B I try to be on friendly terms with people but the truth is that there is always some rivalry involved.
    C I have good friends in the office and it's a shame that sometimes rivalry gets in the way.
    D I treat my co-workers as friends. I am not there to take part in a competition.

6. Which is more important job satisfaction or promotion?

A I want to get to the top. That *is* my job satisfaction.

B I want to be promoted, of course, but it is important to have job satisfaction as well.

C I need to enjoy my job. Promotion would also be nice but it is not one of my main concerns.

D Enjoying the job is what it is all about. Nothing else is that important.

7. Do you define yourself in terms of the job you do?

A Yes, that is totally who I am.

B I like to think there is more to me but I have to confess that I do identify with my job.

C The job is an important part of my life but I do many other things as well.

D I have a full and active life. The job is just a part of that.

8. Which is more important work or family life?

A Work, of course. I am usually bored when I'm at home.

B I try hard to do the best for my family but work often has to come first.

C I try to make sure I do my job well but I must be able to enjoy quality time with the family.

D The job is what I do to keep the family clothed and fed but the family always comes first for me.

9. Do you constantly plan your rise to the top?

A Yes, I have a plan and I am following it to the letter.
B I don't exactly have a plan but I do work towards promotion.
C I do my best and hope that my work gets noticed.
D I don't think about it.

ANSWERS

Score 4 points for an A, 3 for a B, 2 for a C, and 1 for a D

35–40 You are headed right for the top. Nothing else matters to you except cutting a path through the corporate jungle. The good news is that with your level of commitment you can't fail. You'll achieve what you want and you'll find it sooner rather than later. The bad news is that there isn't room for much else in your life. You don't have the time, energy, or inclination to do much about relationships. People who are connected with you in any way can expect to come a very poor second to your career plans. Let's hope that you are never lonely.

25–34 You are ambitious but not completely single-minded. You will do well but may lack the drive to reach the very top. You want to have a career and a life but you might find that juggling the two is trickier than you anticipated. You worry that your family and friends suffer because of the pressures of your work. You also worry that your work suffers when you pay too much attention to things outside it. In short, you are likely to be very stressed and may find it hard to cope.

10. **Are happiness and ambition closely linked in your life?**

A I could never be happy unless I was striving to better myself.
B I do find that doing well at work makes me happy.
C I could be happy without being ambitious.
D I think ambition would get in the way of my capacity to enjoy life.

15–24 You always work hard and would like to get on but you are not obsessed by this thought. Your main concern is to look after your family, lead an interesting life, and do all the things that make life enjoyable for you and your loved ones. Although you will never have an office on the top floor you don't really care too much. You have seen those high flyers and you don't envy them their high pressure lifestyles one bit. You would really like to be able to take it easy and chill out when you want to.

Under 15 Ambition doesn't mean anything to you. It is not that you are lazy just that you feel life is too short to waste on something as meaningless as corporate climbing. You have a family, friends, and interests all of which take up your time. You would not sacrifice any of these for a fat check or the status of being a VIP. Other people make snide remarks about your lack of ambition but you couldn't care less—you are happy the way you are.

CHAPTER 2

EMOTIONAL MOMENTS

Our grandparents wouldn't even have known what the phrase meant but nowadays being "in touch with your feelings" is regarded as one of the essentials of good mental health. We often speculate about what we are feeling and why we feel as we do. This section is designed to study some of these issues, including, how grouchy or insecure we can be (sometimes, without even realizing!). It is a place for you to penetrate your protective layers and find the real god or goddess lurking beneath. Although the tests are often presented in a humorous way they do have a serious purpose. Insight is a hugely important quality (if you have ever met someone completely lacking in this then you'll have seen just what a problem that can be). These questions were written with the object of helping you probe your inner feelings and shine a light into the seldom-visited areas of your inner-being. You will be invited to look at your levels of anger, self-esteem, and vanity, among other things, and to assess for yourself how you feel about your life and the people you share it with.

Are your feelings easily hurt?

The world can be a rough place and people aren't always kind. If you want to live happily it's best not to let yourself be hurt by the things people say. Some of us are better than others at shrugging off mean remarks. This test is designed to tell you whether your skin is as thick as the hide of a rhino or is so sensitive that you break out in hives at the mere thought of a wounding comment.

1. YOUR PARTNER TELLS YOU THAT YOU NEED TO LOSE SOME WEIGHT. DO YOU:

A Pout, then eat a whole bag of cookies to console yourself.

B Feel a bit insulted but then remind yourself that you had been thinking the same thing and it prompts you to do something about it.

C Say, "What about you? If you were standing where I am you'd see just what a fat butt you've got."

2. A FRIEND FAILS TO COMMENT FAVORABLY ON YOUR NEW OUTFIT. DO YOU:

A Feel mortified and decide never to wear those clothes again.

B Feel a bit hurt but, on reflection, decide that you could make some changes to the outfit to make it more acceptable.

C Take no notice and decide that your friend is simply jealous.

3. NO ONE REMEMBERS THAT IT IS YOUR BIRTHDAY. HOW DO YOU FEEL?

A Deeply hurt and it takes you days to recover your good humor.

B Decide that it's not the end of the world. You don't want everyone to know your age anyway.

C Oops! You've forgotten that it's your birthday.

4. YOU OVERHEAR ONE OF YOUR WORK COLLEAGUES CRITICIZING YOUR ATTITUDE. WHAT WOULD YOU DO?

A Confront them and tell them how upsetting these remarks are—if they have a problem with you, they should talk to you directly instead of gossiping.

B Convince yourself that no one really likes this person anyway therefore their opinion will not be taken seriously.

C Appear to laugh the whole thing off but get your revenge later by passing on some juicy gossip about the offender.

5. YOU STAND FOR ELECTION TO THE COMMITTEE OF YOUR GOLF CLUB BUT ONLY GET A HANDFUL OF VOTES. DO YOU:

A Immediately resign from the club. You could never face those people again after such humiliation.

B Tell your fellow golfers that you are happy that you won't have to give up valuable golfing time for dull administrative duties.

C Completely forget you were up for election, don't turn up for the vote, and forget to enquire about the result.

6. YOU TAKE A PART IN AN AMATEUR THEATRICAL PRODUCTION AND THE LOCAL NEWSPAPER MAKES FUN OF YOUR PERFORMANCE. WHAT DO YOU DO?

A Give up acting and stop going out in public for several months.

B Write a letter to the newspaper pointing out that their critic obviously fell asleep during most of the second act.

C Cut out the article, frame it, and display it in your home. At least they spelt your name right and there is no such thing as bad publicity.

7. YOU ARE INVITED TO SPEAK ABOUT YOUR JOB AT YOUR CHILD'S SCHOOL. AFTERWARDS YOUR KID TELLS YOU THAT THEIR FRIENDS THOUGHT YOU WERE BORING. HOW DO YOU REACT?

A You feel really bad and the embarrassment in your child's eyes just about kills you.

B You decide that it's simply a case of kids being little monsters. You soon forget about it.

C You tell your child that no one in that room could possibly have been more bored than you were.

8. SOMEONE TELLS YOU THAT YOU REMIND THEM OF HOMER SIMPSON. YOU REACT BY:

A Going into a major sulk. You can never watch *The Simpsons* ever again —the memory is too awful.

B Laughing it off, tell them you've had a dose of jaundice recently.

C Saying you're delighted. Many people think well of Homer and you are happy to be compared to an international "star."

9. YOUR CLOSEST FRIEND GETS MARRIED AND DOESN'T ASK YOU TO TAKE PART IN THE WEDDING. DO YOU:

A Delete your "former" buddy from your address book. They are dead to you now.

B Shrug it off and look on the bright side—at least you don't have to stay sober at the wedding reception now.

C Make a speech at the wedding party and tell a good joke at your friend's expense, even though you haven't been asked to.

ANSWERS

Score 4 points for an A, 3 for a B, and 2 for a C

35–40
Boy, are you touchy! You'd better toughen up or you're going to spend your whole life being upset. There's no need to take offense at every little thing that people say about you. Sometimes they're just teasing you a little. Even when they do mean to be hurtful why give them the satisfaction of knowing that it worked? It would be much better to ignore their remarks and let them think that they had failed to get to you.

30–34
You need to be less sensitive. You try to avoid feeling vulnerable and you know that you ought to be tougher but somehow you still let people bug you. You should work hard at cultivating a fearless attitude. Remember to walk tall and give everybody the impression that you are full of self-confidence. At first you will have to act a bit, but eventually, you will believe in yourself completely.

10. YOUR PARTNER MAKES FUN OF YOU IN FRONT OF YOUR FRIENDS. DO YOU:

A Stop speaking to your partner and mope around thinking about divorce.

B Wait until the friends have gone and then point out to your partner just how stupid and hurtful the remarks were.

C Retaliate by telling the same friends a really embarrassing story from your partner's past.

25–29
You are self-assured enough to brush off hurtful behavior without much trouble but you still have a sensitive side and people do get to you from time to time. When this happens you manage to deal with it quite well and you don't let anyone really get you down. Your attitude is often very mature and shows a high degree of emotional security.

UNDER 25
You have the hide of a rhino. Nothing is allowed to upset you. This saves you from all sorts of emotional harm, which can be a good thing. The problem is that your toughness is gained at the expense of any sort of sensitivity. You have invested so much effort in making yourself super cool that you find it hard to open up to people. You are wearing an emotional suit of armor and although it protects you, it makes it difficult for anyone to get close to you.

THE MOVING FINGER WRITES...

This little teaser is a great test of your ingenuity.
At first sight it appears impossible but, just like one of
those "locked room" detective mysteries, there is a rational
explanation if you look hard enough. All you have to do is
reproduce the diagram opposite by drawing one continuous
line and without ever lifting your pencil from the paper. The
circle part is easy enough, but what about the dot in the
middle? Clearly there has to be a trick involved but are you
sharp enough to work out how it's done?

Find the answer on page 256.

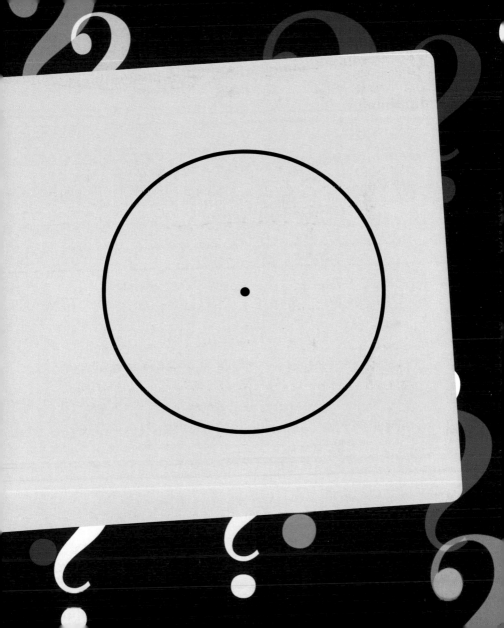

Are you a hypochondriac?

Do you worry about your health? Do you wonder whether every ache and pain might be a sign that the Grim Reaper is coming to take you away? Or are you carefree, letting your body get on with its job while you enjoy life to the max? Whether you're the kind of person who thinks that not using the remote on the TV is exercise or whether your body is a temple, when it comes to health, we all have our own way of dealing with our frailties. Now is your chance to find out whether or not you should be thinking a bit more about your general health and well-being.

1

Do you worry about your health?

A I rarely think about it. What's the point? Doctor's just tell you to stop doing everything that's fun in life. I take every day as it comes.

B I do all the right things. I jog, I diet, and I gave up smoking. If I thought I had serious symptoms I'd visit the doctor right away.

C My doctor knows me better than his own wife. I am constantly making appointments when I have aches and pains just to be sure. It's better to be safe than sorry.

2

Do you regularly find it hard to enjoy activities like drinking alcohol for fear of the effect it is having on you?

A What do you think I am, a Californian? I eat and drink what I like and to hell with the consequences.

B I used to drink with enthusiasm but now I try to stick to recommended amounts, though once in a while I let myself go.

C I never drink alcohol or eat fatty foods. I'm on a macrobiotic diet and am thinking of getting a personal trainer.

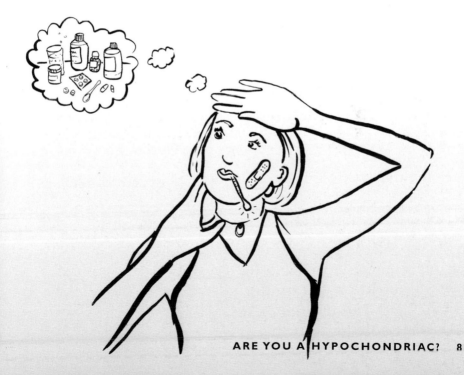

3

Would you consider a headache and slight stomach pain a strong enough reason to visit your doctor?

A Do I look like a wimp? I'd just get on with my work. Headaches always go away if you ignore them.
B I'd take a painkiller and rest a while. If the pain lasted more than 48 hours I'd go see my doctor.
C I'd phone the doctor for an urgent appointment. You can't bee too careful about these things.

4

You visit the doctor, with some minor symptoms. However, he's not convinced that you have a serious illness and suggests rest and a couple of aspirin. Would you accept his diagnosis?

A Yes, he's a trained professional, and knows more about the state of my body than I do. If he says I'm OK, then I'm OK.
B You trust him to some extent, but if I was still worried I'd get a second opinion to make sure.
C I study this sort of stuff on the internet all the time. You think I don't know a serious symptom when I see one? I'd threaten to sue unless he took me seriously.

5

Do you fear that you may have caught the latest superbug if you read about it in a magazine article or saw it on TV?

A No, if you worried about all that stuff you'd go crazy.
B I'm quite sensible and would only be concerned if I really thought there was a strong possibility that the bug I'd read about was one I might have.
C I once convinced myself I had Lhasa fever and I've never been further east than New Jersey.

6

Do you follow the hospital soaps on TV because you pick up useful medical information?

A I never watch them. The doctors and nurses spend all their time making out and ignoring the patients.

B I did learn how to perform the Heimlich maneuver but I'm still waiting for a chance to use it.

C I could get a postdoc with all the stuff I've learned. I think *ER* should be compulsory viewing for everyone.

7

Do you take regular exercise in the hope of lengthening your lifespan?

A I only ever walk as far as the car.

B I belong to a gym but rarely go. I always mean to get more exercise but I'm busy and, to be honest, I don't enjoy working out all that much.

C Whenever possible I run, swim, and pump iron. I walk so much that I've forgotten how to drive.

8

Do you make sure you have regular medical check-ups?

A What, at those prices? Do you think I don't have anything better to do with my money?

B I do get a check-up every few years. It's expensive but it gives you peace of mind.

C I have expensive medical insurance that gives me a check-up twice a year. Who'd begrudge money spent on something so important?

9

How long do you expect to live?

A Who cares? I just enjoy the time I've got. I'd rather die young and happy than end up a vegetable at ninety.

B My family tend to last until their early eighties. If I'm careful I might do the same.

C Die? How am I going to die with all the supplements I take? In any case, if anything does happen I'm being cryogenically stored so that they can patch me up when medical science has found a cure for whatever I've got.

10

On a scale of 1–10 (where 1 is Excellent and 10 is Poor) how would you classify your present state of health?

A How would I know? I never think about that sort of stuff. I guess I'm about a 5.

B I hope I'm quite good—maybe around 6 or 7.

C The amount of trouble I take I should be a 10 but I'm constantly worried that something has snuck up on me while I wasn't looking.

ANSWERS

Score 4 points for an A, 3 for a B, and 2 for a C

35–40 You're going to die—maybe not today, maybe not tomorrow—but soon, and it will serve you right. On the other hand, at least you never worry about your health so maybe you're not as dumb as you look. You really do need to take a lot more interest in your well-being. There is a huge difference between someone who doesn't indulge in unnecessary worry over health and someone who ignores their body until something goes wrong. Go and get yourself checked out. You may find that there are things you need to do to ensure that you stay in good condition.

30–34 You are full of good intentions but could do more to promote a healthy lifestyle. You know it makes sense. The trouble is that you don't ever follow through and turn your intentions into active changes. It is no good knowing that you should be healthier if you don't take the right steps to improve. You must get to grips with doing some exercise, and eating more healthily. Stop putting it off and do it NOW!

25–29 You are a complete health freak. With all the care you take you should be indestructible so long as you don't worry yourself to death. Try to loosen up a little and enjoy life more—it doesn't last forever no matter what you do. You do all the right things but you do them to excess. There is no point in being so concerned about your health that you ignore all other aspects of your life. There is an awful lot going on out there and it's about time you got out into the world and experienced some of it instead of sitting at home counting your vitamin pills.

Under 25 You need help. You're the sort of person who sits outside the hospital all day just in case you get taken ill. This really has to stop because it is ruining your life completely. Everybody has occasional health worries but you have turned what is a perfectly legitimate level of anxiety into a full-blown neurosis. It's time to take control and start living!

Insecure? Not Me!

Are you one of those lucky people who always feel that your life is working out just fine or do you, like most of us, have some insecurities? Are you sure that your friends really like you, that your partner isn't looking for some fun on the side, and that your boss isn't thinking of replacing you with someone younger and cheaper? I can see by your face that some of that hit the mark. Now try this test to find out just how bad things really are.

1. **You discover that your best friend is having a party but, so far, you have not been invited. Do you:**

   A Forget about it. You've known this person for years and are confident that there's no way that they wouldn't invite you.

   B Assume that the invitation is in the post and anxiously wait for it to arrive.

   C Sulk because you are clearly not being invited to the party.

2. **Your partner has to work late several times in just a few weeks. Would you:**

   A Get on with some jobs that need doing around the house. You can always do with a bit of time to yourself.

   B Worry that maybe something is going on behind your back.

   C Hang around outside your partner's office and snoop around. You'll need hard evidence for the divorce.

3. **You go to buy a new outfit. Do you:**

   A Buy something bold and innovative sure in the knowledge that all your friends will accept that you are a trend setter.

   B Ask the girl in the shop what she thinks of the outfit you've chosen.

   C Worry that you've made a bad choice and people are laughing at you.

4. **You finish an important piece of work and send your report to the boss. How do you feel?**

   A Relax! You worked damn hard on that report and the boss will be impressed.

   B You're glad the work is over but not sure about the reception it will get. You start to come up with excuses as to why the work was substandard.

   C You don't sleep. Every word of your report comes back to haunt you. It was a bunch of pretentious waffle and the boss is going to hate it.

5. **Your boss leaves a message for you to see her urgently. Do you:**

   A Assume that she wants to thank you for your hard work.

B Think about the day you sneaked off early to go to the mall.

C Panic! This is it! She's never liked you and today is the day when she's going to fire you.

6. An official-looking letter arrives but it is impossible to see who it's from without opening it. Do you:

A Open it immediately. It's nothing to worry about—probably a tax rebate.

B You put it to one side until you have the courage to open it.

C You write, "Return to sender" and send it back immediately.

7. You find your child and their friend giggling. Do you:

A Try to join in the joke.

B Ignore them, kids are always like that.

C Withdraw with as much dignity as you can. They were laughing at you.

8. A colleague fails to return your greeting. Do you:

A Wait until you see him again and tease him that he's going deaf. Obviously his mind was elsewhere.

B Ask a mutual friend whether you could somehow have offended him.

C Avoid your colleague in future—he obviously doesn't want to know you.

9. You are on a train when you overhear two women talking about someone who looks weird. How do you feel?

A Take no notice. Who cares?

B Look around in the hope of finding out who they're referring to.

C Try to sink into the ground and disappear. They obviously meant you.

10. You enter a room and someone gets up and leaves. Do you:

A Step aside—what's so strange about that?

B Wonder whether the person was trying to avoid you.

C Rush from the room, humiliated. Everyone saw you being snubbed.

ANSWERS

Mostly As You're so secure they could tie a suspension bridge to your left leg. Nothing ever makes you doubt yourself. On the whole your emotional security is a good thing. It certainly makes life quite pleasant for you and for those around you who are encouraged by your confidence. The only problem is that you do come across as a bit too self-assured and some people will find that a bit threatening. We could tell you that some people think you're unbelievably smug but would you listen?

Mostly Bs You are quite secure most of the time but you still have moments when you feel that you are not as well liked as you deserve. Usually you can put these moments out of your mind quite quickly. You go through life with quite a positive attitude and, on the whole, you are able to believe that people love and value you as much as you would like. Without being conceited you have quite a good opinion of yourself and you are not too surprised that others seem to share that opinion. Like everyone, you have the occasional fits of self-doubt but these don't happen often enough to cause you real problems and, when they do occur, you can usually find ways to reassure yourself.

Mostly Cs You're beyond all help but God's. And you probably think that God doesn't like you either. How do you expect anyone to like you when you so clearly don't think you're worth liking? This test, of course, has simply confirmed your worst fears and now you're off to sulk in the bathroom as usual. Why don't you get to grips with this problem? It has blighted your life so far and, if you let it, will blight the rest of your life as well. You should get some help and try to cultivate a feeling of self-worth. You are not nearly as hopeless and useless as you think.

How well do you know yourself?

Some people have the gift of insight and others simply don't. Many of us are acutely aware of our own strengths and weaknesses, recognizing the same traits in others, while there are those who are full of foolish notions about who they are and what they believe. This test is designed to help you to discover which of these groups you really belong to. Do you know your own mind and how to use it? Now is the time to find out.

1. **It has been said that everyone has one perfect partner who they must search for in order to find true love. What do you think?**

A There's no such thing as "the one." It depends on time, circumstance, age, and any number of factors. You take what you can at the time.

B The true love of my life may exist, but there may well be others, too. There are any number of examples of people who have learned to love again after bad relationships.

C Everyone has a chosen mate that they must find in order to experience true happiness, anything else is just a compromise that will leave you unfulfilled.

2. **You invite friends over, they throw their jackets on the nearest chair and don't use coasters! How do you react to this?**

A Tell them that your coffee table is an antique and insist they use the coasters. You take the coats and hang them up yourself.

B Blame your partner for insisting on coasters and try to show that you are far more relaxed and easy going. Leave the jackets where they are, they aren't going to leave a mess even if they do look untidy.

C What's a coaster? And if all that's lying around the room are those jackets then that's a definite improvement on the way it looked yesterday!

3. Do you believe that breakfast is the most important meal of the day?

A Definitely, breakfast sets you up for the day ahead, and ensures you are at your best. You can't have productive day without it.

B You know that breakfast is important and in your heart you want to make sure you have a proper meal in the morning every day, but more often than not you run of the house ten minutes late clutching a cereal bar.

C You never worry about breakfast. You had some Pop Tarts at 2 pm once, but breakfast isn't something you will ever make a habit of.

4. You live in the city and are invited to the country by a friend. Your friend asks if you'd like to go for a walk through muddy fields wearing galoshes, do you accept?

A You are horrified at the thought of anything touching your Armani suit and instead stay behind to read the business section of the newspaper.

B You are not overly keen on the idea of walking through muddy fields, but rather than offend your friend decide to go anyway.

C You go to the countryside to get away from the city and really enjoy the whole experience. You've not done much walking in the countryside but getting muddy sounds like fun.

5. You are invited to a meal at a Japanese restaurant. Much to your surprise your fellow guests all request chopsticks instead of knives and forks, do you follow their lead?

A Yes of course, a different society requires different culinary skills. You have used chopsticks before and are happy to join in.

B Despite your lack of skills using chopsticks, you think that failure to do so is rude and attempt to struggle on anyway.

C You have no problem with your inability to use chopsticks, and are quite happy to request normal cutlery, regardless of what the other guests may think of you.

6. **When you start seeing a new boyfriend/girlfriend, you view them as:**

A A never ending challenge of improvements and alterations to mold them into your ideal.

B A generally suitable person for you, but with some problems and annoying habits that could eventually cause you to break up.

C A good choice for the time being, you aren't thinking long term and for now you're happy enough.

7. **The meaning of life is?**

A To get a good education, find a high paying job, move to the 'burbs, start a family, and hold regular barbecues.

B To try and do as above, but have some fun along the way, not try too hard, and put having a good time before success in employment.

C Just to be happy.

8. You are organizing a school barbecue together with another family. Unfortunately you have contrasting ideas on the theme of the barbecue. How do you go about getting your own way?

A You don't need to convince the other family of anything. Just take no notice of their ideas and continue to make decorations of your own.

B Try to compromise with the other family, discuss ideas and if your plan is actually better, then it might be chosen anyway, and you remain open to what the other family suggests.

C Let them have their stupid barbecue, you didn't care that much anyway.

9. A branch from a tree in your garden overhangs onto your neighbor's property and instead of requesting it be trimmed, the neighbor has hacked off all the branches hanging into his space. The tree now looks ridiculous. Do you:

A Take your saw and go and hack apart some of the greenery in their garden—an eye-for-an-eye, it's only fair.

B Go next door and tell him that his actions were completely over the top and that if he'd actually asked you, you would have been happy to have trimmed the tree. You realize that technically you were wrong, and he had the right to take this action, but that the situation could have been handled better.

C Realize that you're not too bothered, you don't venture in to the garden much anyway, and because you ran over their child's new bike the week before, it was probably deserved.

10. The best description of the state of your basement or attic is:

A A perfectly ordered and, where necessary, chronological storage area of past items that, although no longer needed in the house, are still easily recoverable.

B As above, but although started with good intentions regularly gets to the point where a major clear up is required to sort it all out.

C A dumping ground for unwanted rubbish that has no order whatsoever. It may quite possibly be guarded by a three headed dragon for all you know.

ANSWERS

Mostly As

You are very logical, very practical, and very effective and not at all afraid to admit this. This trait of character is something that is hard to change, and a good organizer is always useful to any partner, or set of friends. However you do show some signs of snobbery and a reliance on social values that may well see you excluded and isolated if you don't tone down.

Mostly Bs

You don't seem to know your own mind, perhaps something along the lines of an A, with some C traits added. While we all have situations where we become lazy and unorganized you might do well to find more definition in your life. If you don't want to use chopsticks, then don't use them! If you don't want your friends putting water marks on the table, then don't let them!

Mostly Cs

Credit must be given to you for being strong, and content enough to freely admit your various failings in organization, but this seems to border on cowardice once too often. If you've worked hard on a suggestion for a barbecue then why give in, your idea might be far better. You need to stop taking the easy route out all of the time and be more confident about your choices.

PULLING THE WOOL OVER YOUR EYES

Here is a well-known nursery rhyme that has been re-written in a strange way. You'll no doubt remember the original version, but are you sharp enough to spot what has been done to change it? This is one of those puzzles that seem obvious once you know the answer, but this was tried on a radio phone-in program and not one listener found the solution. You need a keen eye for detail to spot what has gone wrong with Mary and her lamb. The best way to work it out is to write down the old version and look at the two side by side. Turn to

page 255 for the answer.

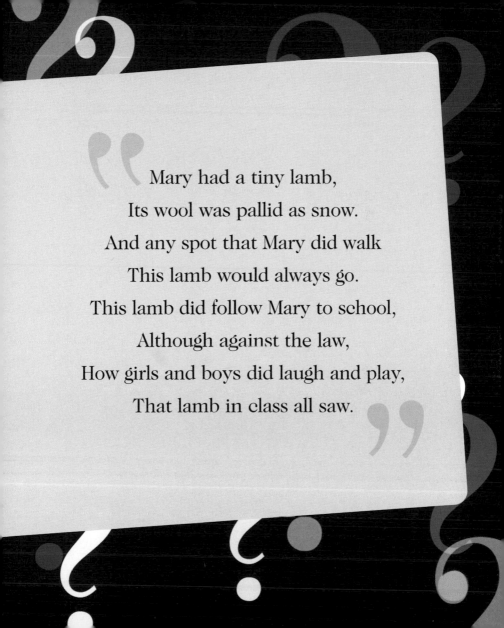

Mary had a tiny lamb,
Its wool was pallid as snow.
And any spot that Mary did walk
This lamb would always go.
This lamb did follow Mary to school,
Although against the law,
How girls and boys did laugh and play,
That lamb in class all saw.

Do you have an inner monkey?

Most of the time we manage to behave ourselves but there are occasions when we just can't ignore that mischievous spirit that we seem to have inside us. We are tempted to do outrageous things just because it would be fun to see what happens. How good are you at resisting this impulse? Are you able to put the "inner monkey" firmly back in its cage or do you give in and have some fun even if it will result in trouble?

1. **IT'S BEEN RAINING HEAVILY. AS YOU DRIVE HOME, YOU PASS THE LOCAL SCHOOL JUST AS ALL THE TEENAGERS ARE COMING OUT. YOU HAVE AN OPPORTUNITY TO DRIVE THROUGH A LARGE PUDDLE AND SPLASH THEM ALL. DO YOU:**

A Put your foot down and give them all a shower! If they were in the car and you were next to the puddle then they would soak you.

B Drive at normal speed so that any splashing incidents are not malicious and you can now feel completely guilt free... sort of.

C Slow down just enough to look as though you made an effort. You'll still catch a few of them with any luck.

D Slow down until you are barely moving so there is no risk of splashing the kids. You have noticed that the traffic lights ahead have turned red and you don't want them coming after you for revenge.

2. **YOUR BEST FRIEND (WHO SHARES YOUR APARTMENT) HAS AN IMPORTANT JOB INTERVIEW TOMORROW. DO YOU:**

A Set all the clocks forward an hour in a hilarious practical joke to make your friend think that they've missed the interview.

B Make sure your friend is up on time but keep making jokes about how they are going to completely fail the interview.

C Plan to wake your friend up and tease them about the interview, but you actually completely forget about it and oversleep.

D Wake up an hour before your friend to make breakfast and send them to the interview in the best possible condition with a better chance of getting the job.

3. **YOU GO OUT WITH A FRIEND TO A RESTAURANT. THEY LEAVE THE TABLE FOR A MINUTE TO TAKE A PHONE CALL LEAVING THEIR FOOD TEMPTINGLY UNGUARDED. DO YOU:**

A Attack their main course with some really hot chili.

B Make your friend paranoid by suggesting that you may have tampered with the food when in actual fact you have done nothing.

C Sneak some of their fries.

D Do nothing. You're too mature to play childish games.

4. **YOU GO TO A MOVIE AND HATE EVERY MINUTE OF IT. THIS IS THE WORST MOVIE YOU HAVE EVER SEEN. DO YOU:**

A Tell everybody that the movie had a really steamy sex scene in it that's not to be missed, when the film is, in fact, a historical documentary about turkish baths.

B Tell everybody the movie was really excellent. Why should you be the only one to suffer?

C Say, "I really hated it but, hey, what do I know?" You're pretty sure that the movie stinks but you'd quite like somebody to share a joke about it with.

D Warn all your friends that this is one movie they should avoid at all costs. You don't want to risk losing friends by sending them to see this garbage.

5. A FRIEND HAS A NEW GIRLFRIEND AND IS ANNOYING YOU WITH HIS CONSTANT TEXT MESSAGING. WHEN HE GOES TO THE RESTROOM YOU NOTICE HE HAS LEFT HIS CELL PHONE UNATTENDED. DO YOU?

A Switch a few names over in the phone's address book. Your friend won't be able to stop laughing when he finds out he's been sending messages to his girlfriend and they've been received by his friend Dave.

B Hold the phone to ransom when your friend returns and threaten to send embarrassing text messages on his behalf.

C Read his messages and have a good laugh at the ones from his girlfriend.

D Leave the phone, it's not his fault that you're bitter and single and that he has a new girlfriend, is it?

6. YOU ARE AT A FORMAL PARTY AND WAITERS ARE COMING AROUND OFFERING DRINKS AND SNACKS. A TEENAGER HOLDING A PLATE WITH A HEAP OF CANDY CONFRONTS YOU. DO YOU?

A Trip the kid as he turns away from you. What a laugh!

B Take a candy from the very bottom and cause a big scene as they all cascade off they tray.

C Notice that the plate is clearly quite heavy and unstable so you take plenty of time before making up your mind as to whether to take one or not.

D Politely and conventionally take one from the top and let him go without torturing him.

7. IT'S EARLY SUNDAY MORNING. NOBODY SHOULD BE UP AT THIS HOUR, BUT THE PAPERBOY IS STRUGGLING UP YOUR DRIVE WITH A NEWSPAPER CONTAINING TWENTY SUPPLEMENTS. DO YOU:

A Let the dog out for some fun. It won't kill him but it barks loudly and will scare him.

B Go out and yell, "Why are you so late? Where have you been all morning?"

C Watch him struggle to fit the newspaper into your mailbox.

D Go outside and take the overlarge newspaper to save him the trouble of fitting it into your mailbox.

8. A NEIGHBOR ANNOYS YOU BY PLAYING LOUD MUSIC DAY AND NIGHT. DO YOU:

A Hire a mobile disco to play outside his house until he begs for mercy.

B Order dozens of pizzas to be delivered to his address.

C Turn your own music up to compete with his.

D Explain to him politely that the loud music is disturbing you.

9. YOU ARE FIRED BY YOUR EMPLOYER. DO YOU:

A Wipe the hard drive of the company computers before you leave.

B Set off the sprinkler system as you go out the door for the last time.

C Phone your ex boss using an assumed voice and tell him he is wanted for questioning at the local police station.

D You leave quietly and get a new job.

10. YOU COME HOME TO FIND YOUR PARTNER IS IN BED WITH SOMEONE ELSE. DO YOU:

A Phone the police and report an intruder in the house.

B Set off the fire alarm.

C Call up the stairs, "Honey, I'm home!" and wait to see what happens.

D Tip toe out of the house. You'll raise the subject at a later date.

ANSWERS

Score 4 points for an A, 3 for a B, 2 for a C, and 1 for a D

35–40 Your inner monkey has just taken over the zoo! You have a mischievous spirit that is totally out of control. While part of you finds this very funny, you must realize that you run the risk of doing something really dangerous just because you can't keep your sense of fun under control. There is nothing wrong with the occasional practical joke but you need to anticipate the results of your actions. You vastly overestimate how funny other people find your little pranks. They do not think that you are an amusing joker, they think you are a dangerous jerk.

25–34 You enjoy playing jokes and do not always understand that others don't share your sense of fun. You do, however, understand that some pranks are just too extreme to be amusing. You shy away from stuff that is dangerous or harmful and that has to be a good thing. Even so you should try walking around in your victims' shoes for a while and consider what it feels like to be at the receiving end of one of your pranks.

15–24 You are quite sensible on the whole. You might very occasionally play a prank on someone but you are not addicted to being a practical joker. People do not have to worry that you will suddenly get involved in some crazy scheme that causes mayhem. Your attitude is very mature but not so mature that you are boring.

Under 15 Your inner monkey seems to have escaped from its cage. OK, so you are always responsible and safe. That is good but it doesn't make you much fun. It wouldn't hurt just now and then to do something to show that you are human. You could just cut loose sometimes and act a little bit wild to show that you have a sense of fun.

How grouchy are you?

Some days you just don't feel that great. You get out of bed feeling uneasy and, even after a shower and some breakfast, the feeling just doesn't go away— you remain grouchy for the whole day. Nothing seems quite right with your life on days like this. But the question is are you like this occasionally or is it a regular problem or, heaven forbid, are you like this most of the time? Here's your chance to see how unfriendly you can be.

1. YOUR PARTNER ACCIDENTALLY SETS THE ALARM CLOCK OFF FIFTEEN MINUTES EARLY. DO YOU:

A Scream, "Turn that damn thing off!" and hide under the quilt.

B Get up grudgingly and spend the extra time enjoying a nice hot shower.

C Snuggle up to your partner and enjoy a little quality time.

2. YOU'RE GOING TO WORK BY CAR WHEN ANOTHER DRIVER PUSHES HIS WAY AHEAD OF YOU. DO YOU:

A Overtake the car, stop, pull open his door, and scream at the driver.

B Honk your horn and make "You're crazy" gestures at him in the mirror.

C Take no notice. There's one born every minute, eh?

3. YOU AND YOUR PARTNER GO TO A RESTAURANT FOR A ROMANTIC MEAL ONLY TO DISCOVER THAT THERE IS A LOUD BUT GOOD HUMORED BIRTHDAY PARTY GOING ON AT THE NEXT TABLE. DO YOU:

A Complain to the management and ask to be moved to a quieter table.

B Put up with the noise. After all, they're only having fun.

C Strike up a conversation with them and join in the festivities.

4. YOU'RE ON A TRAIN WHEN THE PERSON OPPOSITE MAKES A SERIES OF CALLS ON HIS CELL PHONE. DO YOU:

A Give him bad-tempered looks or demand that he turn the thing off.

B Try to ignore him but fume quietly and make an effort to concentrate on your newspaper.

C Barely notice him. After all, how is talking on a phone different from chatting to the person beside you?

5. YOU'RE JUST PASSING A CROWD OF KIDS WHO HAVE COME OUT OF SCHOOL WHEN YOU TREAD IN A LUMP OF CHEWING GUM. DO YOU:

A Give the kids hell. You can see some of the little brats chewing gum!

B Curse inwardly and scrape the stuff off when the kids are out of sight.

C Remove the gum and decide to be more careful where you step in future. The kids? It might not have been their gum anyway.

6. **YOUR NEIGHBORS ARE HAVING A NOISY PARTY LATE AT NIGHT. DO YOU:**

A Phone the police.

B Go round and ask them politely to turn the noise down.

C Go to bed and put in earplugs. After all they don't do it often and they're usually good neighbors.

7. **YOU SPEND TIME PLANING A DAY OUT BUT, WHEN YOU RISE IN THE MORNING, IT'S RAINING HEAVILY. DO YOU:**

A Complain loudly and give everyone around you a hard time because your plans have been ruined.

B After an initial burst of irritation you make new plans for something you can do indoors.

C Cheerfully pull on your waterproof clothing and galoshes and go out. Who cares about a little rain?

8. **YOU GET HOME AFTER A LONG DAY AND FIND THAT YOU ARE HAVING YOUR LEAST FAVORITE FOOD FOR DINNER. DO YOU:**

A Refuse point blank to eat it and storm out to buy take-out.

B Eat enough to avoid insulting the cook but then sneak down later and make a snack.

C Eat up and look like you enjoyed it. After all, the cook spent time and trouble over this food.

9. YOU'RE HAVING A BAD HAIR DAY. DO YOU:

A Spread the misery by criticizing those around you. If you're feeling bad, everyone is going to feel bad with you.

B Keep sneaking to the rest room and try to do something to make yourself look and feel better.

C Tell all your friends and make a joke of the whole thing.

10. A FRIEND FIXES YOU UP WITH A BLIND DATE BUT WHEN YOU GET THERE YOUR PARTNER FOR THE EVENING IS VERY UNATTRACTIVE, TOTAL SQUARE. DO YOU:

A Give your friend a piece of your mind and storm off.

B Suffer in silence because you don't want to hurt anyone's feelings. But you're going to phone your friend in the morning . . .

C Decide to try and enjoy the evening. Who knows, perhaps your date will turn out to have a great sense of humor and a really warm personality.

ANSWERS

Mostly As

Grouchy? You? There are large, carnivorous reptiles with more human warmth than you have. How do you live with yourself? More to the point how does anyone else put up with you? Come on, loosen up! Maybe the world would be a nicer place if you gave it just half a chance. Why not make a point of waking up happy? Think of all the good things in the world and try to be happy about them. You should really make a point of being more patient and tolerant of other people. They are not there just for you to knock about. Try to value them and understand that they, too, have issues and feelings.

Mostly Bs

The question is, are you grouchy at heart but don't have the courage to be as nasty as you'd like to, or are you really a nice person who gets irritated against your better nature? Have some faith in your own niceness and decide to send your crabby alter ego to the back of your mind. People are trying to like you if you'd just give them a chance. What are you afraid of? Do you think that if you take off your mask people will take advantage of you? The truth is that a lot of people find you just a bit scary. You would benefit from having a more approachable manner.

Mostly Cs

Who do you think you are, Pollyanna? You don't have to be so darned nice *all* the time! Everyone is entitled to a grouchy moment sometimes. Try to stop pretending to be a saint and let your human side show a bit—people will respect you all the more for it. Those who are good all the time are usually not being honest about their feelings and unless you are willing to acknowledge that there is an aggressive side to your character you will end up living a lie and that won't be good for your mental well-being.

Could you cope with being rich?

Everyone fantasizes about being rich. People regularly come up with get-rich-quick schemes or buy lottery tickets in an effort to make it into the wealthy "A list." Wouldn't it be wonderful if you could have everything that money could buy? Just think what a wonderful life you'd have if you were financially secure. But would it really be everything you dream of? When you think about it clearly, would you know what to do with all that money? And would it bring you a bright, shiny new life or simply destroy the life you already have?

1

Would you see the inevitable increase in the number of people calling you and trying to make you their best friend as a good thing?

A No, this wealth may come and go, and with it will go the new-found friends. You prefer to stick with those who've been with you from the beginning.

B You'd be wary, though not paranoid, that everyone is out to get hold of your wealth. There must be some genuine people out there.

C This is your key to the kingdom! Now is your chance to mingle with the beautiful people and leave the masses behind!

2

What would your first major purchase or investment be?

A You'd set up trust accounts for the family and donate some money to charity.
B You would set up trust accounts, but spend some of the money on something that you've always wanted.
C Spend! Spend! Spend! You've lived for so long without money that you're determined to enjoy it while it lasts.

3

How do you spend your money at the moment?

A You only spend what you earn and never get in to debt unless it is absolutely necessary.
B By and large you keep to a fixed budget, but a small debt to buy, say, a new car, or pay for a holiday is acceptable.
C You're constantly in extreme debt to ensure that your house is always up to date with the latest luxuries. You're determined to be leader of the pack.

4

Can money buy you happiness?

A No, the money will only drive a wedge between you and those close to you.
B If you have underlying problems money could help, say by giving you and a partner a break and a holiday, but on its own it couldn't possibly repair significant damage to a relationship.
C Of course you're unhappy now! Who wouldn't be unhappy living in a bug-infested apartment!? Once you move to Hawaii you're bound to find happiness.

5

Would you use your money to try and make yourself more respected at work?

A No, this wealth came by complete chance, and it was largely undeserved. Any credit or respect to come from it would be attributed to what you did with it and whether you made good use of it.

B You would be tempted to buy a flashy car and designer suits, but only to enhance the respect you had already gained for all of the hard work you did before you became rich.

C Work? Work's for poor people, I'm rich now!

6

How would money affect the way you treat your children?

A Very little, it is important to learn the value of money early on, and not spoil them, although I would certainly make sure that their path through an increasingly expensive education system became easier.

B You would try not to change their lives too much on a day-to-day basis, but spending a bit more on presents at Christmas and birthdays is only natural, after all you're not selfish and you don't want all the money for yourself.

C You'd spend a large amount of the money on your children. They're bound to love such a generous parent, aren't they?

7

How would money affect your diet?

A If anything it would make you healthier. You'd eat more organic food, and perhaps the money would give you more time to worry about diet and less about trying to earn a living.

B You'd hope to vary your diet more, and use some free time to develop a wider taste in food. You'd take the chance to sample restaurant food more.

C Cooking is for poor people. Now you can afford to eat out nearly all the time.

8

How do you view rich people at the moment, in comparison to yourself?

A A mixture of people, some who have earned their fortune, others who have not, all entrusted with a fragile gift that some are better equipped to use than others.

B A class of people who, despite some wrong turns, have a far superior quality of life to the rest of us. You are quite envious.

C Put it this way—your role models are Michael Douglas and Catherine Zeta-Jones.

9

Would you move your child straight to private school?

A Perhaps, depending largely on the school they currently go to. If you thought that their current school was of a high enough standard, you'd let your child choose.

B Private schools offer a far superior route toward the best colleges, and although you would consult with your child, you would certainly advise them that private schooling would help them.

C There would be no discussion—private schooling for those who can afford it is an absolute must.

10

You get a flat on the highway. Previously you had always changed the tire yourself, would you still do the same now?

A Yes of course, money has not changed you, you're not helpless and you're certainly not afraid to get your hands dirty.

B You may have done jobs like this before, but you never enjoyed doing them. Now you'd call someone out to do the job for you.

C You're rich and important now. You call a repair man, order a cab to take you to your destination, and have your car delivered to you there, later.

ANSWERS

Mostly As

You clearly have both feet firmly planted on the ground, and while you certainly seem capable of being rich, you don't actually seem that keen on it! You frequently refrain from caving in to any of the luxuries that wealth would offer you, and instead seem content to simply enhance your existing lifestyle.

Mostly Bs

You are open to temptation like most people are. While you appear to want to do the right thing and save the majority of the money, you can't lose the little voice telling you to go out and buy that shiny red sports car! There's nothing wrong with that, most people will never have this kind of opportunity so use it to do something that you've always dreamed of. The only question is whether you would be able to balance that with saving the money sensibly.

Mostly Cs

If this is you then I'm sure the red sports car was already in the drive before the voice in your head could even tell you to go and buy it! Ultimately money will make you miserable, you will become complacent living a lavish lifestyle that you will eventually be unable to bankroll, and the fake high flying friends and you have acquired will vanish as quickly as they appeared. Tread carefully.

THE HOLE TRUTH

This is a tricky little puzzle that tests your power to think laterally. Logical thinking tends to plod along one step at a time from basic premises to an inevitable conclusion, but lateral thinking delights in tricky maneuvers that keep you on your toes. In this case the puzzle seems simple enough. All you do is take a piece of stiff card and cut out a hole the size of a small coin (such as a penny). Then take a larger coin (such as a quarter) and push it through the hole. You can handle the card and the coin as much as you like but you mustn't bend or tear the card. This puzzle will not repay a persistent, painstaking approach. You will either see the answer in a flash and laugh out loud at it, or you probably won't get it at all (but that won't prevent you trying it out on another innocent victim). Page 255 will reveal the solution.

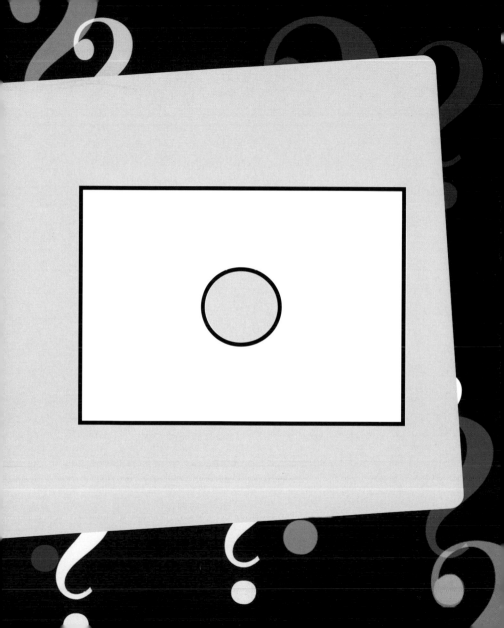

Do you have an inner saint?

Do you feel constantly inspired to do good? Is your life an endless quest to help others or are you quite content to help yourself? Most people like to think that they are on the side of the angels but often, when it comes to transforming those good intentions into actions, they find that they are just too busy. This test will try to uncover whether you have an inner saint. It will separate those who are spurred to action by good causes from those who exist purely to advance their own self-satisfaction.

1. **YOUR LOCAL PLACE OF WORSHIP IS IN A BAD STATE OF REPAIR AND URGENTLY NEEDS RENOVATION. DO YOU:**

A Ignore it. This is not your problem and you don't want to be involved. You only attend services on occasion.

B You suggest that some funds be allocated to a program of renovation. You offer to make a donation.

C You start a campaign to raise funds and give your own time and money to make it a success.

2. YOU ARE UNEXPECTEDLY INHERIT MONEY FROM A DISTANT RELATIVE. YOU ARE SURPRISED TO RECEIVE SUCH A LARGE SUM, AS YOU HAD LITTLE CONTACT WITH HER, THOUGH YOU KNOW SHE HAD A DEEP-ROOTED LOVE OF ANIMALS. WHAT WOULD YOU DO WITH THE MONEY?

A Spend it. This is a piece of good luck for you. Just because the money came as a surprise is no reason to look this gift horse in the mouth.

B Spend some of the money and give the rest to an animal charity, which you believe is what your relative would have wanted.

C Donate the entirety of the inheritance to the animal charity. You would feel guilty spending money from someone you barely knew.

3. YOU HAVE FINISHED YOUR SHIFT AT WORK. IT IS CHRISTMAS AND THE COMPANY IS AT ITS BUSIEST SO YOU ARE ASKED TO STAY AND WORK FOR AN ADDITIONAL HOUR, EVEN THOUGH YOU HAVE NO REAL OBLIGATION TO DO SO. WHAT IS YOUR RESPONSE?

A You refuse because you are anxious to get home. It's Christmas Eve and you want to get back to your family.

B You agree to work the extra hour but demand double pay for doing so.

C You happily work the additional time. It is the season of goodwill after all, so why not get into the spirit of it?

4. YOUR PARTNER PLEADS WITH YOU TO DRIVE HIM TO A PARTY SO THAT HE CAN ENJOY A DRINK. DO YOU SELFLESSLY OBLIGE?

A No, you the hate the couple you're going to see, and only a nice cold beer (or glass of wine, your choice) is going to get you through it. You argue your case.

B You agree, but make a mental note that you drove on this occasion and will bring it up next time.

C It's important to your partner to go to this party and you are happy to oblige. It doesn't matter that you are bored as long as your partner has a good time.

5. WOULD YOU EVER GIVE UP YOUR FAVORITE FOOD (FOR EXAMPLE, CANDY OR BEER) FOR CHARITY?

A No, it's every man for himself! I don't go to work all day and come home not to have a beer!

B Yes, but not for too long . . .

C Of course, compared to the suffering of those in other countries, I could manage a few weeks without candy.

6. WOULD YOU GIVE UP YOUR WEEKEND TO HELP OUT A COLLEAGUE WITH WORK THAT THEY WERE STRUGGLING TO FINISH?

A Why should you? If they aren't up to completing the work, then maybe it's time to look for a less demanding job.

B You'd help but make sure they feel indebted. There will be payback at some time in the future.

C You don't hesitate to offer a helping hand; a good deed is its own reward.

7. WHY DO YOU BELIEVE PEOPLE GIVE MONEY TO CHARITIES?

A Because it makes them feel good about themselves and they can take a tax deduction.

B Both because it makes them feel good, but also for the actual benefit that it will give to the charity.

C Entirely for the benefit it will bring to the charity.

8. WOULD YOU CHEAT TO WIN A GAME OF SCRABBLE?

A Yes, a win is a win regardless of how it as achieved. Besides, cheating at Scrabble is a sort of achievement in itself.

B I admit I've sometimes cheated but I always felt bad about it afterwards. I don't think I'd ever do it again.

C Cheating is despicable. How could I possibly take any pleasure in a victory gained by dishonesty?

9. YOU SEE SOME KIDS STEALING MONEY FROM A BEGGAR. WHAT WOULD YOU DO?

A Nothing. It's not my business.

B I'd chase them away and try to get the money back.

C I would put some of my own money in the collection box when the beggar wasn't looking.

10. YOU ARE ASKED TO GIVE A LITTLE TIME TO A DOOR-TO-DOOR CHARITY COLLECTION IN YOUR NEIGHBORHOOD. DO YOU:

A Refuse point blank. Why should you give up precious time to help people who won't help themselves?

B You are not really willing but you find a refusal too embarrassing. You go out collecting one evening but then you make an excuse not to do any more.

C You agree enthusiastically and spend many happy evenings collecting for this very deserving cause.

ANSWERS

Score 1 point for an A, 2 for a B, and 3 for a C

25–30 Your inner saint is so powerful you probably have a halo. You are the natural ally of the poor, sick, hungry, and dispossessed. Of course, all this activity leaves you very little time to have a life of your own. Maybe if you stopped to consider for a moment, you might wonder whether your own family are missing out as a result of all your good works. Maybe you should cut back on your charitable work a bit and spend some time looking after those closest to you.

20–24 You are well intentioned and really try to do your best for those who need help. You will go to great lengths to help anyone you consider to be less fortunate than yourself. However, you are also aware of the need to look after your own career and family life. You are not so devoted to good works that you are willing to ignore other important aspects of your life. This balanced approach means that you are very successful in both areas of life. Those close to you feel good about your good works while not feeling that they are second best.

15–19 You don't really have much of an urge to help others. You go through the motions and have some good intentions but you are slow to take positive action. The truth is that you are far too concerned about your own wants and needs to give much thought to others, especially if they are people you don't even know. You feel that you should only be expected to take care of close family and friends. You certainly aren't willing to give up precious time to activities that don't bring you any sort of material reward.

Under 15 Your inner saint must have gone on pilgrimage because it is certainly not visible from where we are standing. You really care for no one but yourself. You don't even feel obliged to pretend to any finer feelings. You assume that everyone is out for themselves and you see nothing wrong in this. Even those unfortunate enough to be among your family and friends are not allowed to come between you and the things you want.

Are you always right?

No one enjoys being in the wrong. It's not a thing that's easy to admit but, every once and awhile, we are forced to confess that we have made a mistake. In general, most of us just find these situations embarassing but are able to concede defeat. However, there are some people who simply find it impossible to admit to their errors. They rigidly follow the "never apologize, never explain" school of thought while everyone else round them boils with anger and frustration. Of course none of this applies to you—or does it? Take our test and find out.

1. YOU TRY TO OVERTAKE ANOTHER DRIVER BUT SOMEHOW MANAGE TO SCRAPE AN ONCOMING VEHICLE. BOTH THE OTHER DRIVERS INSIST THAT THE ACCIDENT WAS YOUR FAULT. WHAT DO YOU DO:

A You really hate to admit it but there are two of them and only one of you so you have no alternative but to agree it was your fault.

B You say nothing. Later, when your lawyers get to work, there may be a chance to prove that you were not responsible.

C You try to bluff your way out of your difficulties simply by shouting louder than the others. You are so convinced of your own rectitude that eventually they start to have doubts.

2. A MEMBER OF YOUR FAMILY GETS A JOB IN A VIVISECTION LAB. YOU ARE PASSIONATELY AGAINST ANIMAL TESTING. DO YOU:

A Feel disgusted, but remain quiet about it. They know your views and have ignored them.
B Leave pamphlets that confirm your opinions around the house.
C Have a major argument with the offending family member and try to force them quit the job.

3. YOU SUE SOMEONE AND THE CASE GOES AGAINST YOU. DO YOU:

A Accept the verdict and pay up.
B Appeal, but when you lose you decide it's time to call it a day and grudgingly pay the damages.
C Keep on appealing. It's costing you a fortune but you just know that right is on your side.

4. YOU'RE AT A FAMILY PARTY. IN THE COURSE OF CONVERSATION SOMEONE DISAGREES WITH WHAT YOU'VE BEEN SAYING. YOU'RE TOLD YOU'VE GOT YOUR FACTS WRONG. DO YOU:

A Ignore it. This guy is only a second cousin who no one has seen in twenty years. Who cares?
B Avoid an actual argument but make your feelings clear by making a couple of derogatory remarks about the other person.
C What is family when your reputation is on the line? You let the little creep know just where he stands.

5. YOU ARE DRIVING AND YOUR PARTNER IS READING THE MAP. YOU'RE TOLD TO TAKE THE NEXT TURN ON THE RIGHT BUT FAIL TO DO SO. DO YOU:

A Apologize for your mistake and turn back.
B Turn back but continue to insist that your way would have been quicker in the end.
C Continue driving and insist that you are actually taking a short cut.

6. MISSIONARIES FOR A SECT THAT YOU DISAPPROVE OF CALL AT YOUR FRONT DOOR. DO YOU:

A Say, "No thanks" and close the door.
B Tell them that you disapprove of their beliefs and don't want them to bother you again.
C Invite them in and spend two hours arguing that you know more about the subject than they do and that they've got it all wrong.

7. YOU GET PULLED OVER FOR A MINOR TRAFFIC OFFENSE. IF YOU JUST APOLOGIZE YOU'LL PROBABLY GET OFF WITH A CAUTION. DO YOU:

A Grovel in the hope of being let off.
B Sound like you're sorry without actually admitting to any fault on your part.
C Tell the guy where he gets off. Are you going to let some gorilla in a uniform tell you you're in the wrong? Hell no!

8. YOU'RE DATING SOMEONE NEW AND GETTING ON REALLY WELL WHEN YOU HAVE A DISAGREEMENT OVER POLITICS. DO YOU:

A Skip over this minor blip in an otherwise wonderful evening.
B Seek to find a happy compromise that doesn't involve you backing down too much.
C Launch into a full-blown lecture about how completely wrong they are. No relationship is worth you having to back down.

9. YOU FIND OUT THAT STATISTICS YOU HAVE OFTEN USED TO PROVE YOUR POINT ARE IN FACT WRONG. DO YOU:

A Change your point of view and admit to those that you argued with in the past that you were mistaken.

B Change your point of view but try to make it look like nothing has really changed. This is not a correction of your views merely a clarification.

C Hush the whole thing up. With luck no one else will come across this information.

ANSWERS

Score 4 points for an A, 3 for a B, 2 for a C

35–40 You have so little spine that you could be mistaken for an invertebrate. You'd admit you were wrong even before anyone accused you. It is fine to be fair minded and reasonable but you take it to extremes. The truth is that you rather enjoy being a victim because it keeps you from taking responsibility for your own life. For goodness sake get off your knees and stand up for yourself! If you walk around with a "Kick Me" sign on your back what do you expect people to do?

30–34 You are pretty convinced that you're right but you're also savvy enough to make a few concessions that keep you out of trouble. You know that people who are always right are seldom popular and so you make an effort to show that you really do value the opinions and suggestions of others. This works well in your favor. Others perceive you as being a reasonable person to deal with and they respect you for that.

10.
YOU'RE DOING REALLY WELL AT THE OFFICE AND ARE IN LINE FOR A PROMOTION. ONE DAY YOUR BOSS CASUALLY MENTIONS THAT YOU HAVE MADE A SMALL ERROR AND ASKS YOU TO CORRECT IT. DO YOU:

A Apologize and swiftly put the matter right.

B As above but tell yourself that you are only keeping quiet for the sake of your forthcoming promotion.

C Are you going to let this guy push you around? What would John Wayne have done? Damn straight!

25–29 You are too doctrinaire for your own good. You don't have much time for any opinion other than your own, do you? It would be bad enough if you were always right but the sad truth is that you are really just as fallible as everyone else but are unwilling to admit it. This makes you deeply unpopular with the people who have to deal with you. Why not cut them some slack? It can't hurt to occasionally admit to being wrong, can it? The irony is that if you loosened up people would actually be more likely to take notice of you.

Under 25 You really have no reverse gear do you? Even the Pope is not as infallible as you are. Stubborn, pig-headed, opinionated, and downright single-minded only begins to describe your attitude. All your relationships, whether with friends, family, or co-workers, are based on you telling other people what to do. You simply don't see how much harm you are doing. You can't understand that people resent your attitude so much that they are tempted to do the opposite of what you say even when they know you're in the right. How tragic is that? Unfortunately you are so convinced of your own rectitude that good advice is completely wasted on you. The loss is yours.

CHAPTER 3

LIFE SKILLS

We seldom know how much we are capable of until we are put to the test—sometimes the most unlikely people turn out to have great reserves of strength. The questions in this chapter look at a wide range of everyday talents and ask you to consider whether you think you shine in any of these. For example, are teenagers a closed book to you, or are you one of those people who has a gift for talking to the young and eliciting more than grunts in exchange? Do you faint at the sight of a little blood or would you be willing to stop at the scene of a road accident to help the paramedics treat the injured? Do you find yourself at ease when surrounded by people speaking a foreign language or do you panic and flee to find the nearest group of fellow countrymen? This section puts you into a number of interesting hypothetical situations and asks you to assess how well, or how badly, you think you would cope. You might find that, when you think about it, you have a lot more ability than you give yourself credit for.

Are you independent?

"Group dependency" is the psychobabble term for needing other people around you. Humans are generally quite gregarious but some of us need the constant comfort and support that comes from being part of a group while others are quite happy to be loners. Group behavior is encouraged at an early age to promote social skills. The phrase "they're a bit of a loner" is never meant as a compliment. However, there are many gradations between the person who simply cannot function without friends in attendance and those who find any human company oppressive.

Where do you come on this scale? Answer the following questions and find out.

1. YOU DECIDE TO REDECORATE THE LIVING ROOM. DO YOU:

A Throw a "Decorating Party" and get all your friends to come and lend a hand while you serve drinks and snacks.

B Ask a few close friends to help out and promise to cook them dinner.

C You get your parents to help out.

D You do it all by yourself with only the radio for company.

2. YOUR IDEA OF HEAVEN IS:

A A never-ending party with all your favorite people there.

B A place where you can drop-in on friends and family, and they can drop-in on you, at any time of the day.

C A place where you can meet people or enjoy your own company as you wish.

D A place where you never have to meet anyone unless you want to.

3. YOU HAVE A DAY OFF. DO YOU:

A Plan a trip to the beach with a group of friends.

B Visit an old college friend you haven't seen for years.

C Spend the day with your family.

D Go hiking on your own.

4. **YOU HAVE WORK TO FINISH AND YOU NEED TO STAY LATE AT THE OFFICE. NO ONE ELSE IS THERE. DO YOU:**

A Work as fast as you can. You are uncomfortable working alone and you end up having a coffee with the cleaning person to break the monotony.

B Finish the work quickly and arrange to have a friend pick you up and take you out for a pizza.

C You take your time over the work. It's quite nice to have a bit of time to yourself for a change.

D What's new? You usually spend your evenings like this.

5. **THERE IS AN OFFICE PARTY AND THE BOSS MAKES IT CLEAR THAT HE EXPECTS EVERYBODY TO ATTEND. DO YOU:**

A Offer to organize the whole thing. You love parties.

B Go along and have a really great time.

C You enjoy the evening although you wouldn't want to do this sort of thing too often.

D For you this is Hell. You feel completely out of place and leave at the first possible opportunity.

6. **YOUR PARTNER HAS TO SPEND THE WEEKEND AWAY AT A CONFERENCE. DO YOU:**

A Phone all your friends and arrange a big night on the town.

B Get your best friend to come over and watch movies with you.

C Stay alone but catch a movie that you've been meaning to see.

D Bring home some work that you have been meaning to finish.

7. HOW DO YOU USE THE INTERNET?

A It's a wonderful way to meet new friends all over the world.

B It's a useful work tool that you can also use sometimes for socializing.

C You use it almost exclusively for work apart from sending the occasional social email.

D You have spent the last six months constructing a virus called 666 which you plan to use to bring down all modern technology.

8. YOU ARE DUE TO TAKE A VACATION. UNFORTUNATELY NONE OF YOUR FRIENDS ARE FREE TO COME WITH YOU. DO YOU:

A Shop around for a group vacation that you can join.

B Go by yourself but make immediate efforts to make new friends when you get there.

C Put off going on vacation until a friend is free to join you.

D You would never consider taking friends on vacation as you much prefer your own company.

9. **YOU GET A BIG PROMOTION BUT, IN ORDER TO TAKE IT, YOU WOULD NEED TO RELOCATE. DO YOU:**

A Turn it down. You could never contemplate leaving all your friends.

B Relocate but make great efforts to keep in touch with everyone.

C Relocate and try hard to make a new circle of friends as soon as possible.

D Relocate with ease. You don't have any really close friends anyway.

10. **YOU GO OUT TO ENJOY A DAY ON THE BEACH. DO YOU:**

A Go to the most popular spot and manage to find a somewhat cramped space to settle down.

B Avoid the most popular spots and try to find a quieter one that is nearby.

C Search for a beach that has plenty of room where you can spread out and not be too close to others.

D Trek along the beach until you find the most deserted spot possible.

ANSWERS

Give yourself 4 points for an A, 3 for a B, 2 for a C, and 1 for a D

35–40 You are completely group-dependent and can barely envisage life without friends to support you. This is fine for much of the time but we all have moments when we have to be alone and you just don't cope well with these. Try to build up a little independence so that you are not helpless without your friends. It really is possible, and can even be enjoyable, to do some things on your own. You are almost phobic about your own company and, to avoid future problems, you need to gently accustom yourself to occasional periods of solitude.

30–34 You are very keen on being with other people but you can manage occasional periods alone. You would not be happy in any situation where you had to cope alone for long periods of time. You really enjoy the buzz that you get from others but it would be a good idea to realize that you are a capable and effective person in your own right and that, while you may enjoy companionship, you are quite able to function without it.

15–29 You are not too bothered about being part of a group and, although you are quite comfortable having others around, you also relish your own company. Your attitude is quite balanced and healthy. You will find yourself able to cope well whether you have support from family, friends, and co-workers or not.

Less than 15 You are a loner with little need or desire for human contact. People are an irritant much of the time and you are happier without them. You enjoy tasks that you can work on alone and you have a very good relationship with your computer because it makes no emotional demands on you. Although you are not unhappy in your lifestyle you are not leaving yourself open to the personal growth that can be gained from interaction with others. Could you not try to be just a little more sociable?

Are you squeamish?

If a cut finger makes you feel faint or the sight of a bug in your salad makes you retch then you are most probably quite squeamish. Most of us have something that makes us say, "Ugh!" as we shudder in disgust. So just how squeamish are you? Do you go through life constantly terrified of unpleasant sights and sounds or are you a tough individual who can wade through blood or eat cockroaches for breakfast if necessary. Try these questions to discover your "Ugh" factor.

1

You are working in the garden when you hit your foot with a spade which results in a nasty gash that will need stitches. Do you:
A Sit down feeling faint and call feebly for help.
B Apply a temporary bandage at home and call for help.
C Wash and bandage the wound then drive yourself to the ER to have it stitched.

2

You are sitting on a bus when, quite unexpectedly, the child sitting on your neighbor's lap vomits all over you. Do you:
A Scream, lose it completely, and rush to the other end of the bus while frantically trying to wipe the vomit off with a tissue.
B Try to remain calm, mop up the mess, and put on an obviously fake smile for the mother and child.
C Laugh about it. Tell the mother of all the times that your kids did that when they were little.

3

You find dog poop on your front lawn. Do you:

A Leave it. There is no way you are going anywhere near it. It will be good for the grass.

B Put on heavy rubber gloves and carefully remove it with the aid of a very long pole.

C Pick it up using an old plastic bag and dump it in the trash.

4

You are eating at an expensive restaurant when you come across a bug in the salad. Do you:

A Leave the restaurant is disgust. You will never eat in that place again.

B You call the waiter and get him to take it away and bring you a new salad.

C You push it to the edge of your plate and carry on eating.

5

You are on an airplane when the kid in front looks over the back of the seat at you and starts picking his nose. Do you:

A Let out a cry of disgust that alerts the mother—and everyone else—to your problem.

B Make a ferocious face at the little monster and scare him off.

C Smile pleasantly—all kids do that sort of thing sometimes.

6

You are at a lecture when the speaker's chalk makes a horrible squeaky sound on the board. Do you:

A Clap your hands over your ears, and rush from the room.

B Wince a bit but manage to stay in your seat.

C The noise doesn't bother you at all. Who cares about a little squeak?

7

You drop your ring and when you search for it you discover it has rolled into a pile of dog poop. Do you:

A Call the cops. I mean why do we pay taxes?

B Extract it yourself using a plastic bag. Gag dramatically as you try to wash off the mess.

C Pull it out being careful not to get the poop on your fingers. You wash everything but don't feel bad at all.

8

You are on a trek through the jungle. When you stop for a rest you find leeches have attached themselves to various parts of your body. Do you:

A Become completely hysterical and you have to be sedated before anyone can get close enough to remove the leeches from your body.

B Though shuddering with disgust, manage to hold still while the leeches are removed.

C Calmly whip out the iodine and drip it carefully onto the leeches. That'll show 'em!

9

You are invited to dinner at a foreign embassy. They serve sheep's eyeballs, which are a national speciality. Do you:

A Cause a diplomatic incident by shrieking as soon as the dish is served.

B Make yourself as inconspicuous as possible, managing to avoid actually eating the eyeballs but without giving any offense to your hosts.

C You eat the eyeballs. Why not? It is only protein after all.

10

It is a hot summer's day when you suddenly see that ants are swarming into your kitchen. Obviously there was a nest you weren't aware of. Now there are hundreds of ants all over the room and the winged ones are whizzing around the room. Do you:

A Scream for help until a neighbor dials for the emergency services to come and rescue you.

B Get out the vacuum cleaner and suck them all up as quickly as possible while keeping a safe distance.

C Get rid of them using a brush and pan. You simply sweep them up and throw them out of the window.

ANSWERS

Score 4 points for an A, 3 for a B, and 2 for a C

35–40 You are truly pathetic and you know it. I would say that you make me sick but, if I did, it would probably make you sick. You really need to take steps to toughen yourself up a bit. Watch a few episodes of *ER* on TV and don't hide your eyes every time there is a gory bit. Work hard at being less sensitive to things that disgust you. Your squeamishness is an obstacle to enjoying your life and you need to chip away at it all the time. Keep doing small things that will decrease your sensitivity.

30–34 Though you struggle to keep your "Ugh" factor under control, there are still far too many situations where you cannot overcome your squeamishness. However, you are in a good position to improve. Build on your strengths and try to harden yourself to things that have previously caused you revulsion. You will find that you are basically a strong person who, with a bit of work, can become a little braver. Tell yourself that your fears are foolish and that there is nothing you cannot cope with if you really try.

25–29 You have little trouble with squeamishness. Almost nothing disgusts or upsets you. This is fine but you need to be aware that others can be far more sensitive than you. Try to be understanding of their difficulties. You sometimes cause distress to people more sensitive than yourself by your failure to appreciate their difficulties. Not everyone is able to deal with blood, guts, and roaches with your level of calm.

Under 25 OK, so there is nothing that ever makes you go, "Ugh!" Lucky you. However, you really must make an effort to appreciate the problems others have in this area. When situations arise where your lack of squeamishness is needed, the mature thing to do is to use it to save other more sensitive people from trouble. Picking up spiders and throwing them out of the window is good. Picking them up and throwing them at people who are disgusted by them is just cruel.

Can you talk to teenagers?

Teenagers aren't just a different generation, they are a different race. Their language, customs, and morals are a mystery to most people over the age of twenty. They live among us, however, and some attempt at communication is necessary. No one says it's easy but some people do have the knack of not just exchanging greetings with their teenagers but actually holding simple conversations with them. Are you one of the lucky few, or do you find your teens incomprehensible? It's time to find out.

1. Your son or daughter returns from school, and you ask them how their day was. They respond with several grunts, how do you react?

A Grunt back, you can pick up the language, how hard can it be?
B Try and talk using words from your youth. How much can youth culture have changed in the past thirty years? Your kids will surely appreciate the effort you're making and start a conversation.
C You will not stand for this. While they live in your house and eat your food they're going to live by your rules! Tell them their behavior is unacceptable and that they're going to show more respect to you or pack their bags.

2. You agree a curfew of midnight for them to return home from a night out, they eventually stroll in at 3 am, how do you deal with this?

A Relax, you stayed out late when you were younger. If they don't learn to be independent and cope for themselves now, when will they?

B Tell them that you've been worried sick about them and that they should have at least called you to let you know they were OK.

C Lock the door at 12.01 and make them suffer for their lack of respect for the ground rules you set. It's tough love that's needed here, spending the night in the yard might be uncomfortable but you can be damn sure they won't be late home again.

3. How do you handle the inevitable and unavoidable sex talk with your son or daughter?

   A Recommend sex, it's natural, it's all part of life. Contraception? You never bothered with it and it never did you any harm right?

   B Go through it all frankly and honestly, it's better they learn the facts now rather than nine months later when it's too late for them.

   C Recommend a book at the store and change the subject to the golf tournament you'll be participating in next Sunday.

4. The phone bill comes in. It's far more than you anticipated and the big spender still has her ear glued to the receiver in the other room. How do you react?

   A Just be glad that at least she's popular and seems to be happy, if that's not the best thing that could happen to a teenager then what is?

   B Tell her that you simply can't and won't be footing the bill for her lengthy phone use. You sort out a plan for her to gradually repay you for the money she spent.

   C Ban her from using the phone altogether for a couple of months—that should level out the cost.

5. It is Halloween. The usual gang of teenagers come to your door and you provide them with candy. They throw eggs at your house and car. How do you respond?

   A It's all part of the tradition of Halloween, admire their accuracy from the comfort of your armchair.

   B Open the door and start a heated discussion, you aren't over reacting, you gave them candy so what more do they want from you?

   C Make a grab for the nearest sharp object and come running out of the house and chase them—nobody makes a fool out of you.

6. Your son or daughter is playing loud music. The neighbors have already complained but your cherished offspring have barricaded themselves in their room and locked the door. How do you negotiate?

A Competition is the answer. You get out some rock music and turn up the volume. Once they've been beaten at their own game they will surrender.

B Threaten them with the removal of something they can't do without (TV, radio, or computer) if they don't come out. They know as well as you do that they can't stay in there forever.

C Bang on the door repeatedly, in a triumph of brawn over brain. If all else fails find the appropriate tools to remove the door.

7. You embark upon a family holiday, but you have entirely different ideas about what makes a good time. How do you solve this conflict in interests?

A Be liberal, they're young but seem old for their age, let the kids go off and do their own thing so that everybody's happy.

B Compromise by letting them do their own thing, but take precautions: give them your cell phone number and arrange a place where you will meet them later.

C Tell them they are too young to go out alone and take them on your excursions to historic sights and museums.

8. Your daughter asks your opinion on some clothes she is trying on. You hate them. What do you say?

A Pretend to like them, and then your daughter is bound to respect you.

B Tell her the truth. Say that you are not really that happy, but as long as they aren't distasteful then you will not stop her wearing what she wants.

C Tell her that her clothes are completely unacceptable and choose suitable alternatives.

9. Your kids haven't received the grades at school that they are capable of. What action will you take?

A Grades don't count for anything—you never worried about them, and now you are the manager of the pizzeria you work in! Just leave them to it.

B Talk to them about their grades, but instead of yelling, try to find out what has caused the lapse in work and look for a solution.

C Yell at your kids then send them to their rooms until they have learned the entire dictionary from cover to cover.

10. You buy your kids tickets to a rock concert that you are sure they would love to go to. However, when told you will be going as well they turn the offer down. What is your response?

A You are not upset by their reaction, you aren't young anymore. What sort of self respecting teen would want to go anywhere with you anyway? You really have only yourself to blame.

B You are hurt. You made a big effort to do something they would appreciate and they have pushed you away. You find a corner to sulk in.

C Yeah, like you'd go and buy tickets for one of these new terrible bands anyway. It's filth that's what it is. Use the money to buy a flower pressing kit.

ANSWERS

Mostly As

You are far too liberal for your own good. I mean letting the kids go off on their own with no way of contacting them! What were you thinking!? Anything could happen to them and you probably wouldn't notice for three or four days! You need to get over the idea that you're still one of them. You have responsibilities now and they need some guidance and someone to look up to, not just another friend.

Mostly Bs

You are clearly lying! Sorry Mr or Mrs Compromise but if you are going to say that you have never had the tiniest urge to run down the street, after Halloween pranksters, with a sharp instrument, then you aren't fooling anyone. However, your traits of common sense show that you are on the right track. You know what they are thinking but at the same time you're making an effort to assert some authority.

Mostly Cs

I am almost certain that your child is living in fear of you. Go and find some plutonium, get the flux capacitor working again and come back to the future. It is not 1950 any more—children obviously need rules and guidance but not at the cost of your relationship with them. Try and remember what it was like for you at that age.

THE ANSWER IS OBVIOUS!

People who write puzzles are very fond of a type known as the "kick-self" because, no matter how difficult the enigma looks at first, once you see the answer you will kick yourself. This is one of those. All you have to do is look at the figures opposite and decide what letter should replace the question mark. Your first question, therefore, is, "What do the letters represent?" Maybe, as so often in puzzles, they stand for numbers. If so, where does that leave you? What is the significance of the triangle and the square? You really do have to be careful with puzzles like this that you don't get trapped into being too clever. I promise you that an observant ten-year-old could do this puzzle after only a quick glance. Turn to page 255 if you're feeling elderly!

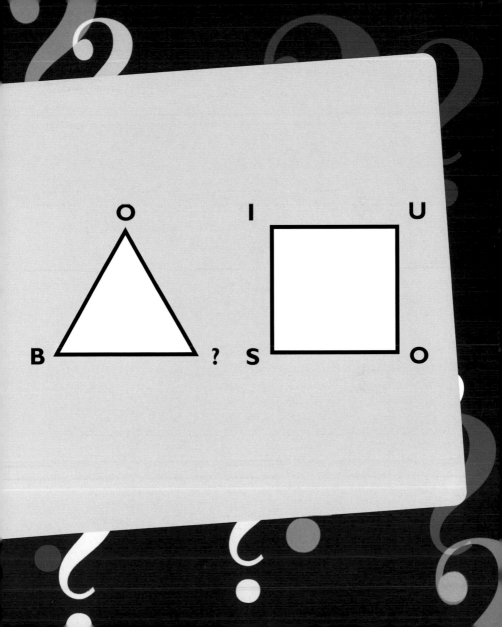

How great is your willpower?

Some people can force themselves to do anything that needs doing. They can get out of bed on the first attempt, go for a five-mile run in the rain, and get ready for work without procrastination. In short, they have willpower. Most of us are guilty of avoiding difficulties, putting off things we find unpleasant, or simply giving up on tasks we find too difficult. How many of us, for example would have the will required to sail single-handedly around the world? This test is to help you find out just how much determination you have. Are you capable of achieving great things or are you one of those who flee anything that looks a bit tricky? Now is the time to find out.

1. **The alarm clock goes off. Do you:**
A Switch it off, hurl the damned thing across the room, then dive back under the quilt and start planning a sick day.
B Press the snooze button and promise yourself that you'll be fine after five more minutes.
C Jump out of bed, pull on your shorts, and go for a nice long run.

2. **How long do you keep your New Year's resolutions?**

A They usually evaporate with the following day's hangover.
B You try desperately hard for at least three days.
C You're still keeping the ones you made when you were eight.

3. **You find a box of cookies you didn't know you had. Do you:**
A Settle down to eat the lot while watching a sitcom on TV.
B Start by eating a couple of the broken ones—which, as everyone knows, have no calories—then work

your way through the others over the next 48 hours.

C Put them back in the pantry and make a mental note to give them to someone else.

4. **Your partner bullies you into going to the gym. Do you:**

A Pretend to go to the gym but you actually sneak over to a friend's house for a couple of hours instead.

B Drag yourself there, make a token effort, and then spend the rest of the time gossiping around the water cooler.

C Really go for it and develop muscles in places where you didn't even know you had muscles.

5. **You decide that you really have to lose some weight. Do you:**

A Order salad for lunch, then change your mind and have the all day breakfast instead.

B Spend three months losing weight and then have a whale of a time

putting it all back on again (and a little extra for good measure).

C Stick to your diet with iron resolve, become Dieter of the Year, and make all your friends hate you.

6. **After some nights of really heavy partying you decide it is time to cut down on your drinking. Do you:**

A Drink white wine instead of red because it contains less alcohol. Then order two extra glasses because, after all, it has got less alcohol.

B Cut down on your weekday drinking but get drunk on the weekend to make up for it.

C Become tee-total but lose all your friends because you are so smug about it.

7. **You go to a party without your partner and someone offers you a bit of "fun" with a very small chance of being caught. Do you:**

A Go for it, then tell yourself that you were drunk and can't be held responsible.

B Refuse but then spend the next six months kicking yourself.

C Refuse and tell your partner the whole story.

8. **You have more work than you can cope with. Do you:**

A Forget about it! They don't pay you nearly enough to worry about that sort of thing.

B Work late for a couple of nights just to look good then tell the boss you need an assistant.

C Work late every night for a week to catch up.

9. **Your parents ask you to turn up for a family celebration that you just know you are going to hate. Do you:**

A Cave in and go to the party. You know that with your family any resistance is useless.

B Come up with a plausible excuse (even though you're fooling no one).

C Explain to your parents that, though you love them dearly, you just can't bear spending time with a lot of boring relatives.

10. **You are very attracted to your best friend's girlfriend/boyfriend. Do you:**

A Make a play for them. After all, you can't help who you love.

B Try to avoid them and hope your infatuation will die out.

C Confess all to your friend and swear that you will overcome your feelings.

ANSWERS

Mostly As

Your willpower is invisible even with the aid of advanced scientific instruments. Unless you try very hard to grow a spine in the near future you are likely to collapse in a gelatinous heap on the floor. Everybody comes across tasks they find difficult or unpleasant but most of them make the effort to overcome their own resistance. Why not make a point of training yourself to follow through on things you find difficult? You could start with small jobs (a visit to your mother-in-law, for example) and work your way up to tasks that require real determination, like filling in your tax form.

Mostly Bs

You are full of good intentions but, let's face it, your willpower cracks under even moderate strain. Try cold showers and early morning runs to build character. The alternative—which is not attractive—is to get used to being a bit pathetic. Do you want that? Of course you don't! There really is nothing wrong with you except that you don't realize how strong you can be. Every time you look in the mirror you should remind yourself that you are really a capable and determined person who never stops until the job is done. If you say it often enough you will eventually come to believe it.

Mostly Cs

You have a will of iron and nothing—but nothing—will crack your resolve. Unfortunately all your friends hate you because you constantly make them look bad and remind them painfully of what a bunch of wimps they are. There is nothing wrong with being a strong character but do you have to make such a show out of it? People don't really mind that you have such enormous willpower but they do object to the smug way you use it to highlight the failings of others. Give everyone a break why don't you.

Can you kiss and make up?

Because frustrations and disagreements are an integral part of life we spend much of our time involved in quarrels. Sometimes it's no more than a brief difference of opinion but occasionally we get into a major argument that causes a serious rift with those nearest to us. Some people are good at recovering from these incidents and are happy to forget them and continue as before. Others find it more difficult and suffer from lingering resentment. A few are completely unable to forgive and forget and will harbor a grudge for years or even decades. Try our test to see which category you fall into.

1. WHAT IS THE LONGEST TIME YOU HAVE STAYED ANGRY WITH ANYONE?

   A A couple of hours.
   B A couple of days.
   C Longer than a month.
   D I never really got over it.

2. YOU HAVE JUST COOKED A BIG MEAL FOR YOUR FAMILY BUT THEY TURN THEIR NOSES UP AT IT. WOULD YOU:

   A Ignore their hurtful comments. They normally enjoy your cooking.
   B You feel hurt but you recover within a day or so.
   C You are seriously displeased. You don't speak to them for a week.
   D You are mortally offended and vow that you will never cook for them again—how could they be so ungrateful?!

3. **YOU ARE WITH FRIENDS WHEN YOUR BOYFRIEND/GIRLFRIEND TELLS A STORY ABOUT SOMETHING DUMB THAT YOU DID. WOULD YOU:**

A Join in the laughter. You know that it was meant in fun.
B Laugh in front of your friends but then refuse to speak to your partner when you get home.
C Retaliate immediately with a story of your own.
D Hold a grudge. When you finally break up you will use this incident to throw back in their face.

4. **ONE OF YOUR CO-WORKERS GETS OUT OF TROUBLE BY SHIFTING THE BLAME FOR HIS MISTAKE ON TO YOU. WHAT DO YOU DO?**

A Ignore the incident. It was a genuine misunderstanding.
B You forgive him but are always slightly wary of him in future. This is not a guy to turn your back on.
C You wait for a chance to get him alone and then tell him exactly what kind of pond scum he really is.
D You appear to have forgotten the incident but are really just waiting for an opportunity. Revenge is a dish best served cold, right?

5. **YOUR MOTHER HAS ALWAYS FAVORED YOUR YOUNGER SISTER TO YOU AND YOUR SISTER HAS ALWAYS MADE THE MOST OF IT. DO YOU:**

A Accept it with a shrug. People feel how they feel, what can I tell you?
B Try to take no notice but it really rankles. Every now and then you can't help making some spiteful remark about it.
C Try to get over how unfair this situation is but your relationship with your mother and sister are seriously damaged.

D Get angry. They don't want you? OK, you don't want them either. After a time you stop speaking to them.

6. YOUR PARTNER HAS A CASUAL FLING WITH SOMEONE AND THEN COMES CRAWLING BACK BEGGING FOR FORGIVENESS. WHAT DO YOU DO?

A You quite literally kiss and make up. You are totally convinced that the remorse is genuine.

B You make up but make sure you keep them on a very tight rein in future.

C You go for a trial separation. If you still have feelings for each other six months from now you might get back together again.

D Hit the road, Jack (or Jill)! And don't you come back no more!

7. YOU DISCOVER THAT A BUSINESS PARTNER HAS BEEN DOING DEALS ON THE SIDE AND CHEATING YOU OF YOUR SHARE. DO YOU:

A Face him with the evidence. Yell at him for a while but eventually decide that he's learnt his lesson.

B You confront him. Eventually you agree to keep the partnership going but make it clear you will be checking everything from now on.

C You end the relationship. How could you ever trust the scumbag again?

D You sue the miserable specimen for his last dime. No one crosses you and lives to tell about it.

8. YOUR PARTNER TELLS YOU THAT YOU'RE GETTING FAT AND HAVE LET YOURSELF GO RECENTLY. DO YOU:

A Take it as constructive criticism. Feel grateful for the chance to change before it's too late.

B You know that it's true but you can't help blaming the messenger. You decide to change but still feel lingering resentment against your partner.

C Boy, are you mad! You're not going to get over this in a hurry. And what about all your partner's faults? Are you supposed to remain blind to them?

D This is the end. Pack your bags and get out of there.

9. A NEW FAMILY MOVES INTO THE HOUSE NEXT DOOR. THEIR DOG KEEPS GETTING INTO YOUR GARDEN AND DIGGING UP THE LAWN. DO YOU:

A Say nothing and hope the dog gets bored of ripping up your garden. You don't want to get off on the wrong foot with your neighbors.

B Go over and ask them to keep their dog under control. Having got that off your chest you invite the family over for a barbecue to try to improve the relationship.

C Have a row about the dog and don't speak to them for months. Eventually you manage patch things up.

D You call the dog warden and have the animal taken away. Your neighbors never speak to you again.

10. ONE OF YOUR TEENAGE CHILDREN IS ARRESTED FOR THEFT AND IS FINED AND PUT ON PROBATION. DO YOU:

A Explain how serious this is. Let them know just how ashamed you are of what they've done. But then you agree to leave it behind you and move on.

B As above, but you find that in future you never quite trust your kid the way you once did.

C You are furious and in future you watch them like a hawk.

D You can never really put it behind you. Eventually a permanent rift develops between you.

ANSWERS

Mostly As
You have a very forgiving nature but you have to be careful not to take it too far. Some people are all too willing to take advantage of you. Try to have a more realistic view of those around you and do not automatically assume that they are acting from good motives. You find it hard to be tough on others but sometimes people need a firm touch.

Mostly Bs
You are quite balanced in your attitude. On the whole you would rather be forgiving, but you are not afraid to take a tougher line when it is called for. You know that people can do bad things but you prefer to think well of them for as long as possible. You show a real maturity and a good understanding of how relationships need a variety of approaches in order to make them work.

Mostly Cs
You tend to be rather judgmental and, though you will resolve quarrels eventually you are often reluctant to do so. Your view of others is quite cynical and you tend to distrust their motives and feel that they will take advantage of you whenever you let your guard down. This rather tough attitude is potentially damaging to you and those around you. Why not try to ease up a bit? Sometimes people respond better to the carrot than the stick.

Mostly Ds
You are one tough cookie. You find it almost impossible to forgive others and this must have a really damaging effect on yourself and those around you. Maybe there is some incident in your childhood that accounts for your lack of forgiveness. Perhaps your parents were overly strict and demanding. In any case, you would be well advised to work on this aspect of your personality. People aren't all angels but they aren't all devils either. A bit of balance would save you a lot of heartache.

Do you have *je ne sais quoi?*

The trouble with *je ne sais quoi* is that, unless you already have it, there is very little chance of acquiring it or even understanding exactly what it is. That indefinable sense of style infuriatingly eludes analysis and while it settles comfortably on the shoulders of some people wrapping them in an unmistakable aura of OK-ness, it obstinately refuses to visit others no matter what they do to encourage it. You can't buy it, earn it, or gain it through hard work. You can't even get it by imitating those who already have it. But the following test will establish once and for all whether you are one of the favored few.

1. **Although you can't get *je ne sais quoi* by imitating others that has never stopped anyone from trying. To what extent do people copy your dress sense?**

A Whatever I wear is what everyone else wears next week.
B Yes, my clothes do invite admiring glances and some imitation.
C I choose clothes that are comfortable and inexpensive. No one ever copies my look.

D You want the truth? If anyone found themselves wearing the same as me they'd probably commit hara kiri.

2. **You are given a piece of antique Chinese silk by an elderly relative. Do you:**

A Effortlessly twist it into a highly desirable accessory that makes your friends green with envy.
B You find a way to wear it and a few people call it "interesting."

C You find a way to wear it and people give you strange looks.

D No matter how hard you try you can't find a way to wear it that doesn't look as though you found it in a dumpster.

3. You want your home restyled. Do you:

A Discover a struggling young interior designer from Ulan Bator. Within weeks her design for your apartment is in all the magazines. She makes a fortune and you are covered in glory for having introduced her to the fashionable world.

B You pay to have the job done by a very fashionable designer. Sadly she is the same one everyone else is using this season. Your apartment looks great but not unusual enough to excite much comment.

C You do it yourself and make an excellent job of it while saving loads of money in the process. People speak kindly of your efforts but don't copy them.

D You do the job yourself relying heavily on cream paint and beige fabrics. Your friends refrain from comment of any sort.

4. You go to a club where you meet an unsigned band that you like. Do you:

A Immediately phone a friend in the music business who signs them on the basis that if you think they're good they must succeed. Within a few months they are topping the charts.

B You tell all your friends about them. Eventually they are discovered and do really well. You then boast about how you knew them before they were famous.

C You tell all your friends about them and find that you are in fact the last to have heard of them. They've already been quite famous for months among people who are really in the know.

D You tell all your friends about them. Your friends tell you that you need your head examined. The band is never heard of again.

5. Are you invited to restaurant openings, film premieres, etc., because you will confer an aura of glamour to the occasion?

A I hardly get a night to myself. If people want me they have to invite me months in advance.

B Yes, I often get invited though, to be honest, not to A list events.

C I'm quite well known locally. If something is kicking off in my neighborhood I always get invited.

D I spend most evenings at home with a good book.

6. You write your autobiography and attempt to get it published. What happens?

A There is a bidding war between several publishers who are desperate to have you on their list. The book is an international sensation.

B You have no trouble getting published and the money they pay you is not bad. The book does not perform quite as well as you hoped but well enough to avoid embarrassment.

C You get no offers and eventually have to self-publish. Your family and friends all get copies for Christmas.

D You self-publish but don't dare give anyone a copy. Your stock stays in your garage for many years.

7. You are a convert to a Chinese sect that preaches enlightenment through various esoteric practices. What happens?

A Your involvement gets the sect mentioned in all the best magazines. Soon membership is huge and you are often asked to speak about the benefits you received from joining.

B The sect becomes better known as a result of your membership. Sadly, as a direct result of some of your comments several of your fellow members are ruthlessly persecuted in various parts of the world.

C Your membership excites no particular interest.

D You make statements on behalf of the sect that are widely ridiculed in various sections of the press. Eventually the founders of the sect ask you to leave.

8. You decide to get away from it all by buying a small property in some out-of-the-way country area. What happens?

A There is a rush to buy other property near yours. Soon all the people you know at home also have holiday houses nearby. The local residents all hate you and wish you would leave.

B Some people copy you. The price of property in the area rises a bit and the locals are quite pleased that you moved there.

C No one really takes much notice of where you live.

D No one could care less whether you are alive or dead.

9. You meet a struggling young writer who is broke and homeless. You are impressed by his talent and want to help so you ask him to come and stay with you rent free until his first book gets published. What happens?

A Not only does his writing flourish but your *je ne sais quoi* rubs off on him. Soon he is the literary sensation of the year and you are showered with glory as his patron.

B The relationship works well at first and his writing is successful but eventually he moves out and tells people that you are holding him back from achieving his true potential.

C The writer doesn't do very well. He blames this on the stifling influence that you have had on him.

D The writer never completes his novel. Years later he still inhabits your spare room and you can't get rid of him.

10. You take up playing the glockenspiel. What happens?

A It is soon the coolest sound around. Glockenspiel music is fast becoming the new craze amongst those with discriminating tastes.

B There is a brief surge of interest but it is soon forgotten.

C No one feels moved to take any interest at all.

D People howl with derision at anyone wanting to play such an obviously unfashionable instrument.

ANSWERS

Score 4 points for every A, 3 for every B, 2 for every C and 1 for every D

35–40 You not only have *je ne sais quoi*, you probably have *va va voom* as well. Everyone is entirely captivated by whatever you do, whatever you wear, and all the places you go. Naturally you are the subject of considerable envy and not a little loathing. Try not to rub it in quite so much. People hate to be reminded that not everyone can match your high standards. If you manage just a little modesty then you will attract deep admiration, but if you lord it over everyone else you must expect them to dislike you deeply.

25–34 Though not a high priest of *je ne sais quoi* you are by no means to be ignored. As long as you don't mind being on the B list you will always get respect and admiration. Could you improve and join the A list? It's possible but not likely. Somehow, very few people manage to acquire any more *je ne sais quoi* than they were born with. You could try imitating people who are even more stylish than yourself. You might just get away with it.

15–24 Not only do you not have *je ne sais quoi* but you will never get it no matter how hard you try or how long you live. Give up all hope now so that at least you won't be disappointed later. The good news is that by no means everyone in the world is concerned about these matters. Many, many people go through life neither knowing nor caring whether they have this mysterious "x-factor." In fact they think that people who worry about this kind of stuff are sad and shallow. You could pretend to be one of these people.

Under 15 You actually manage to possess negative quantities of *je ne sais quoi*! A horrible thought occurs: your sense of style might be so bad that one day people will decide that it's good and you will become an icon. However, this will not happen in your lifetime or, with any luck, in ours.

Would you take revenge on your ex?

Sadly, relationships break up and, when they do, they often leave bitterness in their wake. People who feel wronged by their ex often dream of taking some form of revenge but fortunately they don't often get around to doing anything about it. Tempers cool and most of us eventually learn to forget even if we don't forgive. But there are always a few who simply can't forget and who do travel the dangerous road to revenge. Could this be you? The questions that follow will give you a chance to see how far feelings of anger and betrayal might push you.

1. YOU DISCOVER YOUR PARTNER HAS BEEN HAVING AN AFFAIR. DO YOU:

A Attempt to run down the cheating rat in your car.

B Take your ex's car to the dump.

C Take your ex's clothes and give them to a charity shop.

D Leave a sharp note saying that you expect them to move out before you get home.

2. A FEW WEEKS AFTER THE SPLIT YOU FIND YOUR EX HAS MOVED IN WITH SOMEONE ELSE. DO YOU:

A Send a note to the IRS telling them that your ex's tax returns have been less than honest.

B Confront the newcomer and fill them in on some of your ex's less lovable traits.

C Give your ex hell on the phone.

D Tear up all your old photos. This person is no longer part of your life.

3. YOU BUMP INTO YOUR EX OUT ON A DATE WITH SOMEONE NEW. DO YOU:

A Start a fight with your rival.

B Ask your ex, "Is that the best you could find?"

C Tell them they deserve each other.

D Stop them in their tracks with a fearsome stare.

4. YOUR EX'S BOSS PHONES UP, CLEARLY UNAWARE THAT THE DOMESTIC ARRANGEMENTS HAVE CHANGED. DO YOU:

A Give him a lurid account of your ex's behavior with particular reference to sexual immorality.

B Explain that you have separated and give him your ex's new contact details.

C Say that your ex is out but that you'll say that he called.

D Say your ex is unavailable and offer to pass on a message. You don't want everyone to know about your private business.

5. YOU MEET SOMEONE NEW. DO YOU?

A Tell them the full story of your recent separation with particular reference to your ex's role as #1 Love Rat

B Explain that you only recently separated from your previous partner and are feeling bruised by the trauma you suffered.

C Keep referring to your ex repeatedly in conversation.

D Make light of the whole thing. You know people hate hearing about ex partners.

6. YOU AND YOUR EX FILE FOR DIVORCE. DO YOU:

A Hire the toughest, meanest lawyer in town to destroy your ex's reputation and, with any luck, obtain a financially favorable settlement.

B You hire a tough lawyer but only go for the money. You don't want to cause your ex any serious emotional damage.

C Get a lawyer to look after your interests but make it clear that you don't want any more than you are reasonably entitled to.

D Try for an amicable "no fault" split.

7. YOUR EX WANTS CUSTODY OF THE KIDS. DO YOU:

A Grab the kids and take them where no one will ever find you.

B Fight tooth and nail for custody in the courts.

C Accept that your ex has custody so long as you have access.

D Go for an amicable resolution where you get unlimited access in return for not being a pain in the butt.

8. YOUR EX GETS A JOB AT THE SAME COMPANY AS YOU AND IS OFFERED A MORE SENIOR POSITION. DO YOU:

A Try to undermine their authority by spreading unfavorable stories.

B Appear cooperative but secretly undertake little tasks to undermine their position.

C Adopt a policy of non-cooperation.

D Put your personal hurt to one side and try to get along on a professional basis.

9. YOU HEAR THAT YOUR EX'S NEW RELATIONSHIP IS ON THE ROCKS. DO YOU:

A Phone him up to gloat.

B Tell all your friends.

C Keep quiet but secretly enjoy their discomfiture.

D Feel genuinely sorry that things didn't work out.

10. YOU ARE GETTING MARRIED AGAIN. DO YOU:

A Send your ex an invitation to the wedding.

B Tell everybody and make sure that the news gets back to you-know-who.

C Ignore your ex completely. That part of your life is now over.

D Phone your ex and suggest that you put your differences behind you. Ask them to come to the wedding as a friend.

ANSWERS

For every A give yourself 4 points, a B scores 3, a C scores 2, and a D scores 1

35–40
What a psycho you turned out to be! No wonder your ex left you. You're petty, vengeful, immature, and downright nasty. How do you live with yourself? More to the point, how do you expect anyone else to live with you? Unless you do some serious work in the growing up department you can look forward to a lifetime of failed relationships (not to mention the jail sentence you might get if your revenge attempts get out of hand).

25–34
You try to keep your vengeful spirit under control but, let's face it, you fail far too often. When will you get the message that the person most injured by revenge is you? Your ex has made a break and isn't coming back. Time to move on! By hanging around in the background and trying to attract attention by being spiteful you are just making yourself look ridiculous to everybody who knows you. Quit while you can.

15–24
You are really quite mature and you know how to handle a difficult situation well. You are in an excellent position to wipe the slate clean and get on with your life. Maybe your next relationship will work out better. Certainly you appear to be the sort of person who can bring a lot of emotional maturity into your dealings with a partner. Let's hope things work out well for you. You certainly deserve a break.

Under 15
You don't have a vengeful bone in your body. That much is good. But don't you feel that you are just a bit too understanding and forgiving? It is fine to have a forgiving nature so long as you can get tough when the situation demands it. If you don't change you will continue to be abused by a succession of partners who take advantage of your emotional soft center.

Are you a night owl or an early bird?

The world is full of divisions—rich and poor, fat and thin, smart and scruffy—but few generate such intense emotion as the split between those who thrive on late nights and those who like to get an early start in the morning. No two groups of people find it harder to understand each other. You'd hope that with all the other troubles in the world this difference of attitude could be safely brushed to one side. You would hope in vain. Night owls think that early birds are boring, uptight, and obsessed with their health. The early birds think the others are decadent and dissolute. It is almost impossible for people from either side of this divide to live and let live. This test won't tell you which group you belong to (you must know that already), but it will give you the chance to give your prejudices against the other group a good workout.

1

The phone rings at 9 pm. You say:

A "Who can it be at this time of night?"
B "Great, that must be someone phoning to invite me out for the evening."
C "If I stop to take that I'll be late for the party I'm going to."

2

You are busy at the office and are asked to work late. You say:

A "OK, but I'll be tired tomorrow."
B "No problem, 10 pm isn't very late by my standards."
C "Great, I can go straight into town after I've finished and catch a late movie."

3

You're going on vacation but to catch your flight you need to get up at 5 am. You say:

A "That's no problem, though I'll miss my usual early morning run."
B "I can do it but I wouldn't want to make a habit of it."
C "The only way I'll do this is if someone feeds me coffee every fifteen minutes."

4

You think the birds' dawn chorus is:

A A wonderful way to wake up in the morning.
B A nuisance because it wakes you too early.
C A charming thing to hear just as you come home and prepare for bed.

5

Is 7 am:

A The time you sleep until on Sunday.
B The time you set the alarm for when you need an early start.
C A time you have rarely experienced in a conscious state.

6

Midnight is:

A Well past your bedtime.
B About the time you start to think of going home.
C The point where the party really starts jumping.

7

On New Year's Eve:

A You go to a party. It won't hurt to have the occasional late night.
B You stay up until well past midnight and join in the fun.
C You are to be found the following morning having breakfast at a café that caters to people on the early shift. You haven't been to bed.

8

People who regularly stay out late are:

A Undisciplined and decadent.
B Good fun, though you couldn't keep up with them all the time.
C The life and soul of the party.

9

People who are in bed by 10.30 pm are:

A Sensible and responsible.
B A bit boring.
C You're putting me on. No one really goes to bed at that time, do they?

10

Everyone is supposed to get eight hours' sleep. You say:

A I couldn't function properly without my full eight hours.
B I can do with less sleep for a while but I have to catch up every now and then.
C Eight hours!? What a waste of time. I'll sleep when I'm dead.

ANSWERS

For every A give yourself 3 points, for every B you get 2 points, and for every C 1 point

25–30

It is no surprise to you that you are one of the early birds. You feel strongly that early rising is a symptom of a healthy well-ordered life in which work, rest, and play are kept in perfect balance. You disapprove strongly of people who burn the candle at both ends. You probably find that you can get all your best work done in the early morning before the phones start to ring and other people make demands on your time. You appreciate the peace and quiet and find that it inspires you and makes it easy to think clearly about the tasks that lie ahead of you during the day.

18–24

You are aware of the need for sleep but you also like to have a good time and you enjoy late nights. Your life is spent trying to keep some sort of balance. It isn't always easy. You'd hate to go to bed early all the time but you admit that sometimes you overdo the partying and get a bit run down as a result of lack of sleep. The problem is that over time you run up a "sleep debt" and this eventually has a detrimental effect on your mental and physical performance. You should try to get a bit of sleep now and then to help redress the balance.

Below 18

You are an unashamed night owl who thinks that sleep is for wimps. You pride yourself on your ability to stay out until all hours. You've no objection to a short sleep in the day time in order to catch up but, on the whole, you see being asleep as a waste of your precious time. You think that people who need a lot of sleep lead boring lives and have only themselves to blame. You may be one of those unusual people who simply don't need much sleep. If that is so, then you are lucky. But it is also possible that you are depriving yourself of sleep that you do need and that, eventually, your body and mind will take revenge on you. Be warned, not many people can survive and remain healthy on the tiny amount of sleep you consider normal.

Are you practical?

Let's face it, some of us are just made for practical tasks and others are not. If you can strip down the washing machine and find out why it's making that unsettling rattling noise, or can unblock drains, or produce a delicious meal from a collection of unpromising-looking leftovers, then this quiz is for you. On the other hand, if machines all hate you and the simplest of tasks turns into a lethal battle between you and the hostile world of inanimate objects, then the questions below will only serve to confirm your deepest fear that you are not in the least way practical.

1. YOU MOVE INTO A HOUSE WITH A LARGE BACKYARD THAT IS A BIT OVER-GROWN. DO YOU:

A Embark upon an ambitious program of landscaping that transforms the yard into the envy of the entire neighborhood.

B Initiate a program of landscaping that is only partially successful. Somehow it never quite turns out the way you hoped it would.

C You have a go at the garden but soon realize that it is beyond your ability to do much with it. You cut the lawn and put planters full of flowers everywhere. It looks quite good.

D You go for the natural look—untouched by human hand. You tell people that it is a sanctuary for wild life.

2. THE WASHING MACHINE FLOODS THE KITCHEN. DO YOU:

A Mop up the flood and fix the problem. You've done this before and it's no great crisis.

B You mop up with no trouble but then spend hours trying to fix the machine. You finally succeed and get to bed at 2 am.

C You wrestle with the repair for hours, get to bed at 2 am, and then phone the plumber the following morning to come and fix it properly.

D You slosh about for a while, lose your temper, and phone the plumber.

3. YOU HAVE THE OPPORTUNITY TO BUY A RATHER RUNDOWN HOUSE AT A BARGAIN PRICE. DO YOU:

A Buy it, fix it up, and then sell the house for a huge profit in two years' time.

B Buy it, attempt to fix it up, and sell the property for a small loss.

C Buy it, fail to fix it up, and fail to sell it.

D You don't buy the house. You buy a property that is already in good condition.

4. YOU DECIDE TO TAKE UP CARPENTRY. YOU WILL SAVE YOURSELF BIG BUCKS. DO YOU:

A Take to it as though it was what you were born for. You have a natural gift in this area.

B Study hard and practice for years. The results are not bad though you're not up to professional standards.

C Work hard at it and enjoy yourself hugely. Your friends are very kind about your efforts.

D You enjoy buying all the tools but after two hours you put a chisel through your hand and end up in the ER. Your carpentry career is over.

5. **YOU ARE DRIVING HOME WHEN YOU GET A FLAT. DO YOU:**

A Get out and fix it. It's not exactly hard is it?
B Try to fix it but find that you don't have the right tools and can't get the wheel off.
C Make a token effort at fixing it (so you don't look like a complete wimp) before calling for help.
D Call for help straight away. What do you pay AAA for?

6. **YOUR PARTNER GOES AWAY FOR A WEEK. YOU DON'T USUALLY COOK. DO YOU:**

A Manage perfectly well. Cooking is just common sense really.
B You get out a recipe book and follow the instructions. The results are edible if not orthodox.
C You have a hell of a time trying to cook and fail miserably. After two days you give up and decide to eat out.
D What was take-out invented for?

7. **SOMEONE BUYS YOU AN EXPENSIVE CAMERA AS A PRESENT. DO YOU:**

A Learn to use it with ease. Soon you are producing wonderful photos that are the envy of your friends.
B You attend a class in photography and, after some months, are quite competent. You recognize that you will never be any better than that.
C You take hundreds of photos some of which are not that bad at all, in your opinion.
D Most of your pictures are obscured by part of your thumb.

8. YOU INHERIT A FINE PIANO FROM A WEALTHY RELATIVE. DO YOU:

A Take lessons and find that you have a natural talent for music. Within a year or two you are being asked to perform in public.

B Take lessons and find that you have no natural talent but you work hard and become an almost competent player. You are advised not to perform in public though.

C You get a DIY book and try hard to master it. Eventually you can play *Chopsticks* without more than three mistakes.

D You use the piano as a nice place to display family photos.

9. THE LOCAL AMATEUR DRAMA SOCIETY ASKS YOU TO BE IN CHARGE OF THE SCENERY IN THEIR PRODUCTION OF *THE SOUND OF MUSIC*. DO YOU:

A Accept and make a wonderful job of it. Your scenery is so realistic the audience can almost smell the mountain air.

B Accept and do your best. The result is not at all bad, though one of the mountains does collapse during "My favorite things."

C You make an excuse and duck out of the job.

D You can't think of an excuse so you bribe some kids from the local high school to come along and help you. The result is not too bad.

10. YOU HOLD A BARBECUE FOR ALL YOUR FRIENDS. DO YOU:

A Cook with great ability and complete confidence. The secret of your barbecue sauce is eagerly sought by everyone who's tasted it.

B Cook with moderate ability and complete confidence. Everybody burns the odd sausage, don't they?

C Cook with almost total incompetence and utter panic. The results look like the aftermath of the Great Fire of London.

D You get someone else to cook but try to look like you're helping.

ANSWERS

Score 4 points for an A, 3 for a B, 2 for a C, and 1 for a D

35–40 You're totally at home with practical tasks. Everyone turns to you in times of crisis because you know exactly what to do and how to do it. You may not be much of an ideas person but no one has a better grasp of what it takes to turn ideas into reality. Your only problem is that, with such a wealth of talent, it is hard to decide what areas you should concentrate on. What a problem to have!

25–34 You try hard at practical tasks and make up in effort what you lack in natural ability. People are always glad of your help. If you have a problem it's that you are not always aware of or acknowledge your limitations. It would be safer to decide that some tasks are simply beyond your range of competence. However, you can be justly proud of many of your achievements. People tend not to remember your mistakes.

15–24 Practical matters are not really your province. You have five thumbs on each hand and two left feet. Console yourself with the thought that you are more of an ideas person. Don't struggle to become a practical whiz, just accept that some things are not meant to be. As long as you don't make the mistake of pretending to be practical people won't judge you too harshly. Be honest and tell them that you're a klutz. Everyone will be just fine with that.

Under 15 What can I possibly tell you that you don't already know yourself? You do not possess a single practical bone in your body and probably never will. Steer well clear of all hardware stores. In any case there is nothing to be done. Resign yourself to a lifetime of bills from the people you will have to hire to do all the practical tasks in your life.

PRACTICAL MAGIC

Some people say, "I'm no good at puzzles because they're so artificial. I prefer practical problems." OK, try this. Put a small coin in a saucer making sure it is near the edge. Then pour in some water so that it just covers over the coin. Your task now is to move the coin without spilling the water or getting your fingers wet. Opposite is a list of objects you could use (you don't need all of them, some have been included deliberately to cause confusion). Turn to page 255 for the answer.

a small tumbler

a paper clip

a walnut shell

some dried peas

a piece of paper

matches

Are foreign languages all Double Dutch to you?

In our increasingly interconnected and multicultural world it is more essential than ever to be able to communicate with people from a variety of backgrounds. Even so there are many people who simply don't get on with foreign languages. Some of us just don't see any point in learning a foreign tongue, others would like to learn but find the going is tough. Where do you stand on the issue? Are you able to get by with languages or do they leave you speechless? This test will sort out the polyglots from the tongue-tied.

1. **Most people know at least a few words of other languages. How many languages do you have a smattering of?**
A Five or more.
B A couple, maybe.
C Only one.

2. **Can you translate the following: a) Comment ça va? b) Ciao! c) Auf Wiedersehen.**
A All of them.
B Two of them.
C Less than two.

3. **You are sent a letter in a language you don't understand. Would you:**
A Try to use knowledge of other languages to puzzle out the gist of the message.
B Buy a phrase book and attempt to work out what the writer was saying.
C Throw it in the trash. How are you supposed to understand something like that?

4.You are on a long journey and feeling bored. There is a foreign magazine left by a previous traveler. Do you:

A Amuse yourself by flipping through it trying to work out some of the easy words. You are surprised just how many you recognize.

B You leaf through the magazine and recognize a few words but on the whole it means little to you.

C You don't bother. You know you won't understand it anyway.

5.You are in a foreign country and suffering with a toothache. Do you:

A Find a pharmacy and, using a mixture of language and gestures, manage to buy what you need.

B You find a pharmacy and mime to the assistant until she understands you.

C You find the pharmacy (eventually) but cannot make anyone understand what you want.

6.You go to an authentic Chinese restaurant with friends. Do you:

A Order with confidence. You don't actually speak Chinese but you can bluff your way through.

B You order by pointing to the relevant names and reading them out in a faltering voice.

C You order using the numbers on the menu.

7. A stranger knocks at your door. He speaks a language you don't know. He seems very agitated. Do you:

A Discover that, although he is Venezualan, he can speak Spanish. You are able to help him.

B You manage a few words in Spanish. He asks to use your phone and you let him.

C You close the door. He could be dangerous!

8. You want to go on holiday to Spain. Do you:

A Sign up for an evening class in the language.

B Buy a phrase book and take it with you.

C Expect everyone to be able to speak English.

9. You go to sign up for a part-time language class only to find that Beginners' Japanese is the only one with vacancies.

A You sign up with enthusiasm. You've always wanted to speak Japanese.

B You sign up but stop going after a few weeks. You find it too hard.

C You don't sign up. Learn Japanese? You don't even like sushi.

10. You are offered a big promotion but it would mean moving to the company's office in Bogota. Do you:

A Grasp the opportunity. You already speak Spanish and you'd love for your kids to learn it as well.

B You take the job but find speaking Spanish a bit of a trial. You long for the day they move you back home.

C You turn the job down. There's no way you'd ever manage in Spanish.

ANSWERS

Give yourself 3 points for every A, 2 for every B, and 1 for every C

25–30

You are a natural linguist and enjoy every opportunity to communicate in other languages. You have the courage to try communicating even when you are not confident of the language you are working in. Like all good linguists you don't let minor difficulties get in your way but use every trick in the book to get your message across. You inspire those around you to attempt foreign languages because you make it look easy and enjoyable. Your kids are already ahead of their class in Spanish.

15–24

You are no monoglot but you are one of those people who find languages quite difficult and sometimes you are not really up to the challenge. Instead of plunging in and trying to communicate in any way that works you worry too much about whether you are getting all the grammar and pronunciation correct. Consequently you don't get as much fun out of languages as you could and you don't get the best results. Even so you have potential and, if you keep persevering, you will improve eventually.

Under 15

You don't have the first idea about foreign languages and what's more you don't care. You are the sort of person who thinks that the way to communicate with foreigners is to yell at them in English very slowly. Little do you know that because of your caveman attitude you are depriving yourself of some very rewarding experiences. If you took just a bit of trouble you could learn enough of a foreign language to communicate and it would open up a whole world that you did not even suspect existed. It's really up to you.

CHAPTER 4

FANTASY FILES

There are some things that we fantasize about but are never likely to experience. Some things sound like fun but, if you stop to consider the reality, they might turn out quite differently from the way we expect. For example, everyone thinks they would like to date a superstar, but would you really enjoy it? Imagine trying to have a conversation with someone whose ego is the size of the Grand Canyon. How much fun would it be? This section is devoted entirely to considering situations that we can only dream of and what we would do if dreams ever came true. In reality a lot of the things that seem interesting and fun in our fantasy lives would be troublesome and irritating if they ever really happened. This is your chance to see how your fantasies would look in the cold light of day. Maybe, after giving it a bit of thought, you might decide to eliminate some. On the other hand, you might think that your fantasies still represent what you really want out of life and you need to spend some time pursuing them.

Would you change places with someone else?

We have all met or read about an individual, or seen them on TV, and envied them their looks, money, or lifestyle. It is this sort of envy that has inspired countless stories where, by some means or other, the characters exchange lives. It is the stuff of everybody's fantasies but would you really want to do it? Are you actually so dissatisfied with who and what you are that you would want to change places with someone else? And if so who? What sort of person would you like to be if you were able to choose? Try this test to find out.

1. HOW MUCH DO YOU ENJOY BEING WHO YOU ARE?

A I'm pretty satisfied really, though there are one or two things about myself that I wouldn't mind changing.

B There are quite a few changes needed before I would be really happy with myself.

C I absolutely hate being me. I would love to have the chance to change.

WOULD YOU CHANGE PLACES WITH SOMEONE ELSE?

2. WOULD YOU LIKE TO BE MORE ATTRACTIVE THAN YOU ARE NOW?

A No, I'm not too bothered about my looks.

B I'd certainly like to change some of my features. There's plenty of room for improvement.

C I avoid mirrors. How would you like a nose like mine?

3. ARE YOU ATTRACTED BY THE IDEA OF BEING RICHER?

A Everyone would like to be wealthier but I wouldn't change my identity just for money.

B Money would certainly motivate me.

C I'm desperate to get out of the poverty trap that is my life.

4.

WOULD A MORE EXCITING LIFESTYLE ATTRACT YOU?

A I don't rate excitement that highly. I enjoy the life I have.

B A bit more excitement would be welcome.

C There are funeral parlors that are livelier than my life. I long for excitement.

5. **DO YOU HAVE SOMEONE IN MIND THAT YOU WOULD SWAP PLACES WITH?**

A No, this is the first time I have given it much thought.

B There are a couple of people that I envy and would like to swap with.

C I see people all the time who are better off than me in all sorts of ways. I'd swap with any of them.

6. **WOULD YOU WANT TO SWAP BRIEFLY OR FOR A LONGER PERIOD?**

A A short holiday would do me.

B I think I'd probably enjoy myself so much I'd keep it up for quite some time.

C If I get a new identity it's mine. You want it back you'll have to fight me for it.

7. **SUPPOSE YOU COULD ONLY CHANGE PLACES IF YOU PAID FOR IT. HOW MUCH WOULD YOU BE WILLING TO PAY?**

A Not much. I'm not fanatical about this idea.

B I'd happily give a year's salary to be the person I want to be.

C I'm not rich but I'd sell a couple of major organs if necessary to raise the cash.

8. **DON'T YOU THINK THAT WHEN YOU FINALLY MADE THE CHANGE YOU MIGHT BE DISAPPOINTED?**

A What, "the grass is always greener" sort of thing? Yes, you could be right.

B I'm fairly confident that I would have a good time.

C I can't imagine wanting to be anyone less than I want to be me.

9. **DON'T YOU THINK THAT AFTER A WHILE YOU WOULD FEEL "HOMESICK" FOR YOUR OLD PERSONALITY?**

A Yes, and quite quickly too.

B I'm not sure. I don't think I'd miss being me too much.

C Emphatically not. I'd never want to see my old self again.

10. **DO YOU THINK THAT SUCH A SWAP WILL EVER BE A POSSIBILITY?**

A No. This is strictly the stuff of fantasy.

B I live in hope. One day it might just be possible.

C I think about it all the time. It must be possible somehow.

ANSWERS

Score 1 point for an A, 2 for a B, and 3 for a C

Below 15
You are totally comfortable with who you are. Even the fantasy of place swapping is meaningless for you because you simply don't need that sort of escapism. Your identity is very stable and you have the very clearest idea of who you are and what you are worth. Your self-esteem is sufficient for you not to need a fantasy life in which you are someone else.

15–19
You are quite balanced on this issue. You certainly don't hate yourself and any desire that you have to be someone else is based on simple curiosity. If there were ever a real chance of swapping places you would almost certainly pass it up. You enjoy playing the fantasy game of place swapping but would find the reality disturbing and completely unnecessary.

20–24
You aren't a very happy bunny but you aren't in any real danger. You should try to concentrate on thinking positively about your personality and your life. You are not totally negative about yourself but you do tend to dwell on your faults rather than look for your good points.

25–30
You have real problem, don't you? The degree of self-loathing you display is quite remarkable and not a little dangerous. Most people manage to find something likeable about themselves and their lifestyle but you seem to see your life as a prison from which you need to escape. This is quite an alarming thought. You should talk to someone about these feelings before they do you some real harm.

Would you enjoy eternal youth?

The idea of being able to remain eternally young has obsessed people for thousands of years. There are stories of the Fountain of Youth, which spouts water that confers eternal youth on all who drink it. The alchemists of old sought the philosophers' stone not just so that they could turn base metal into gold, but because they believed that it would enable them to live forever. We all have our regrets about ageing and have occasionally thought that it would be great if it didn't have to happen, but have you ever thought about what that would really be like?

1. WOULD YOU BE PREPARED TO OUTLIVE ALL YOUR CONTEMPORARIES?

A Yes, no problem. I'd get used to it.

B I can see how it would be difficult but it I'd get used to it.

C Immortality is attractive but it would be very hard to leave everyone behind. I'm not sure that I could do it.

D I couldn't do this. It would break my heart to see everybody die.

2. DO YOU THINK YOU WOULD BE ABLE TO FIT INTO THE SOCIETY OF THE FUTURE?

A I'm very adaptable so I'm sure I could fit in.

B It would be a challenge. I'm sure I would have problems but hope I could overcome them.

C I think adapting to the future would be very hard indeed. I'd try but I'm not sure how successful I'd be.

D I think it would be a nightmare to live beyond my own time. I couldn't do it.

3. ANY RELATIONSHIPS YOU MADE WOULD, FROM YOUR POINT OF VIEW, BE TEMPORARY. WOULD THIS BOTHER YOU?

A People come and people go. No problem.

B I can see how you might get attached to people but I'd make it a rule to break off a relationship before they got too serious.

C I think I'd find this very hard. I'm not really into shallow relationships.

D I couldn't do this. I'm always committed to relationships.

4. WOULDN'T LIFE GET BORING? JUST HOW MANY RE-RUNS OF *THE WALTONS* COULD YOU STAND TO WATCH?

A I'm sure I'd find lots of other things to do. I don't see boredom as a problem.

B I think I'd manage as long as no one made me watch the re-runs of *I Love Lucy*!

C I'd be bored at times but I'd put up with it for the sake of all of the advantages.

D I'm sure that boredom would be a major problem.

5. YOU'D HAVE TO HIDE YOUR YOUTHFULNESS OR YOU WOULD SOON BECOME A SUBJECT FOR SCIENTIFIC INVESTIGATION. WOULD ALL THE RUNNING AND HIDING BOTHER YOU?

A No, I'd just become very good at covering my tracks.

B It would be a nuisance but I think I'd be able to manage.

C I'd hate running and hiding. Maybe it wouldn't turn out like that.

D It would be a nightmare. Who'd want to be regarded as a freak of nature?

6. WOULD YOU USE YOUR IMMORTALITY TO BENEFIT HUMANITY?

A Yes, I'm sure I would be able to do things that would help people.

B I'd certainly like to try.

C I'm not sure that being immortal would give me any special way to help people.

D I don't see how I could help. I think immortality would probably make me selfish.

7. HOW WOULD YOU SPEND ALL THAT TIME?

A I'd try lots of new hobbies, see hundreds of different places, and live a whole host of different lives.

B I'd like to become a scientist and use my longevity for the good of humanity.

C I'm not sure but I hope that I'd find plenty to occupy me.

D I really don't know. I think it would be overwhelming.

8. SUPPOSE YOU COULD TAKE SOMEONE WITH YOU, WHOM WOULD YOU CHOOSE?

A I wouldn't like to be stuck with one other person forever. I'd prefer to be alone.

B I might take my partner, but what if we got sick of each other after 100 years?

C I'd like to be with my whole family.

D I don't want to be with anyone because I really don't want to live forever.

9. WOULDN'T IT BE LONELY BEING THE ONLY IMMORTAL?

A No. I'd meet loads of people over hundreds of years.

B I suppose you would miss the people who died, but you would always be meeting new ones.

C It would be a bit weird having to get used to new people all the time. I mean, in a way, they'd all have a "use by" date, wouldn't they?

D Of course it would be lonely. You'd be completely on your own among millions of people with whom you really couldn't connect.

10. WOULD YOU REALLY WANT TO GO ON FOREVER, OR WOULD A FEW HUNDRED YEARS BE ENOUGH?

A I'd want to keep going for a long, long time. In fact I can't imagine a time when I'd actually want to die.

B I think that eventually I might have had enough but it would take thousands of years to get to that point.

C I think I'd get bored of it quite quickly.

D The whole thing sounds like a nightmare to me.

ANSWERS

Give yourself 4 points for an A, three for a B, 2 for a C, and 1 for a D

35–40 You're really into this, aren't you? While you are certainly confident and adventurous to a fault, you are also utterly self-centered and narcissistic. You really don't care much for anyone else and you tend to treat other people like objects. It is fortunate that this is only fantasy because, if you were able to make your dream come true you would probably find that it is not nearly as enticing as you suppose. An eternity without any meaningful human contact would eventually come to seem like a prison sentence even to someone as self-involved as you are.

25–34 You seem to have some grasp of the difficulties of the situation but you are still dazzled by the prospect of a magical life of endless youth. You haven't really thought it all through and you are consciously or unconsciously avoiding some really horrendous problems. Your attitude is rather immature and, if this possibility was for real, you would probably end up blundering into a situation that was way outside your ability to cope.

15–24 You have obviously given this some thought and you can see many of the disadvantages. Even so you are not completely convinced that the idea is a bad one. You have not entirely rid yourself of a romantic notion that eternal youth would be fun. If you were ever given the chance to try this out for real there is still some part of you that would be tempted to go ahead.

Under 15 You have obviously thought this one through and see quite clearly that eternal youth would be a sort of living hell. Because you value your relationships you understand how dreadful it would be not to be able to relate to other people at all. You are mature enough to understand that life is not just about you and your appetites. If the opportunity arose to make this fantasy real you would reject it out of hand and without the slightest trace of regret.

Could you be a castaway?

We all know the fictional story of Robinson Crusoe who was marooned on a desert island. In reality, and more recently, there have been stories of Japanese soldiers who hadn't heard that World War Two was over and continued to live on tiny Pacific islands for years. Have you ever thought what it might be like to be stuck on an island and unable to get off? This quiz will help you find out whether you would love or loathe such an adventure.

1. **You find yourself washed up on a desert island. What is the first thing you do?**
   A Swim back to the wreck of my ship to get essential supplies.
   B Strip and get a tan. I wonder if coconut milk works as sunscreen?
   C Look for a McDonalds.

2. **You need to build a shelter. What would you do?**
   A Bring back timber and canvass from the wrecked ship and build a shelter.
   B Use palm branches to make a hut.
   C Dig a hole in the sand.

3. **You are hungry. What are you going to do for food?**
   A Make a spear and go fishing.
   B Make a bow and arrow and scour the island for game.
   C Search the shore for any tin cans that have been washed up from the ship.

4. **You see a storm brewing out to sea. What do you do?**
   A Find some high ground well away from the sea, dig a pit, cover it with

branches, and go into hiding until the storm passes.
B Wait in my hut for the storm to pass.
C I remember something about taking shelter under a tree. Maybe that would be a good idea.

5. **You are desperately thirsty. What would you do?**
  A Use some plastic from the ship to trap condensation.
  B Try to make a device for distilling sea water.
  C Boil sea water and try to condense the steam on a rock.

6. **You see wild pigs roaming among the trees. What would you do?**

A Dig a deep pit and cover it with branches. Lure a pig onto the branches and—wham!—roast pork for dinner.

B Make a spear and chase the pigs until I managed to catch one.

C Do pigs make good pets?

7. **You find some strange berries growing in the woods. What would you do?**

A Leave them alone. They could be poisonous.

B Watch to see if anything eats them. If the birds are eating them I'd try just one. If that did me no harm I would slowly try eating more.

C See if they taste good?

8. **You need to try to escape from the island. What would you do?**

A Keep a fire burning at all times.

B Scan the horizon for ships.

C People usually put messages in bottles, don't they?

9. **You find a human footprint in the sand. What would you do?**

A Be very careful. I want to see this guy before he sees me.

B I'd try hard to find the owner of the footprint. Any company would be better than none.

C I'd hide. I'm not about to share my coconuts with anyone.

10. **A ship arrives. You're rescued! What now?**

A I'd write a book and sell the film rights to Disney.

B I'd go back to my family and pick up my life where I left off.

C Can I take my pet pig home with me?

ANSWERS

Mostly As

You could have been born on an island! Your survival skills would ensure that you thrived until rescued even if you had to wait for years. You have what it takes to find food and water, protect yourself from the elements and, eventually, contact a passing ship and get rescued. You would find the whole experience a great adventure and would probably be able to write a best-selling book about it upon your return.

Mostly Bs

Like most people who have never had to survive in the open you would struggle at first. There is no doubt that the going would get rough but, after a few initial setbacks, you would develop the skills needed to survive. You might well suffer but you wouldn't ever give up and it is highly likely that you would survive the experience. You probably wouldn't ever actually enjoy living on the island and, once you had been rescued, you would take great care never to get into such a situation again.

Mostly Cs

Here's some friendly advice: never go to sea. Your chances of surviving on a desert island are close to nil. The only question hanging over your island experience would be, "Will you starve before or after you are eaten by wild animals?" You are someone who cannot live without the comforts of civilization, even a walk in the country leaves you filled with dread at the sight of nature in the raw.

THE BEST ROUTE?

This is a puzzle that will challenge your ingenuity. At first sight it might appear to be another problem for those with good visual reasoning skills but it has a broader appeal than that and will yield to the application of a little logic. Some will find that a few trial doodles on a piece of paper will reveal the best way tackle this problem. All you have to do is reproduce the diagram below using as few continuous strokes as possible. You may go over a line twice if you want.

You can begin and end wherever you like.

Turn to page 254 for the solution.

Could you work wonders?

Our whole culture is built on the "can do" principle. We are taught from childhood that we can achieve anything that we want, all we have to do is want it enough and then try, try, and try again. It all sounds good but we know that the reality is not quite so simple. Sometimes the mountain is just too high to climb—unless you happen to be one of those really exceptional people who let nothing get in their way. Are you? Try our quiz and find out.

1. YOU INHERIT A HOUSE FROM A DISTANT RELATIVE. IT IS VERY RUN DOWN BUT, WITH A LOT OF HARD WORK, IT COULD BE TRANSFORMED. WOULD YOU:

A Borrow every cent you can get hold of, mortgage the property, and then put every ounce of effort into renovating it and you eventually sell the house at a huge profit.

B You don't feel you can commit all your resources to this one project. Suppose it doesn't work out? You decide to risk a proportion of your savings and work on the house in your spare time.

C You wouldn't invest much in such a risky venture. You put right the worst of the problems and then sell the house for what you can get.

D You sell the house just as it stands. You don't get much for it but you have risked nothing and made a few dollars quite easily.

2. YOU ARE INVOLVED IN A TRAFFIC ACCIDENT AND ARE VERY SERIOUSLY INJURED. THE DOCTORS SAY YOU'LL NEVER WALK AGAIN. WOULD YOU:

A Refuse to accept their advice. You spend all your time researching new treatments and trying to get yourself mobile again. You have no idea whether you will succeed but nothing will stop you from trying.

B You are profoundly depressed by the doctors' advice but don't give up. You get a second opinion. You are hopeful that one day a cure will be found.

C You accept the situation and do your best to adapt to your new circumstances.

D You have no hope of a cure and cannot accept what has happened to you. Eventually you sink into lethargy and despair.

3. YOU COME HOME FROM A HOLIDAY TO FIND THAT YOUR NEIGHBORHOOD HAS BEEN FLOODED AND YOUR HOUSE WRECKED. WOULD YOU:

A Get the neighbors together and make a plan to clear up the mess. You become the chief organizer and work tirelessly to put your neighborhood back as it was.

B You are overwhelmed by what has happened but, even so, you offer to help in any effort to rebuild the neighborhood.

C You simply can't see how the damage can ever be repaired. You feel duty bound to make some efforts but don't feel very confident that things will ever be back to normal.

D You save what you can and start up a new life elsewhere.

4. YOU WIN $50,000 IN A COMPETITION. WOULD YOU:

A Use this money to launch your own business venture. You've always wanted your own company but have never been able to get hold of the cash.
B Invest the money in high-yield ventures. These are quite risky but, if you're clever enough, you may make a lot of money.
C Put the money in the bank and watch it grow.
D Spend the money on a new car and a luxury holiday.

5. YOU ARE WALKING BY A RIVER WHEN YOU DISCOVER A NUGGET OF GOLD IN THE WATER. NO ONE KNEW THIS RIVER WAS ANYWHERE NEAR A SEAM OF GOLD. WOULD YOU:

A Spend all your time and energy looking for more gold. You start to find large amounts so you give up your job and take up prospecting full time. You make a fortune.
B You come back to the river regularly and look for more nuggets. You find a few and are quite pleased with your efforts. You consider trying to find more gold but decide it is too risky to devote much time to such a venture.
C You occasionally take friends to the river and show them where you found the gold. It makes a good story. People suggest that you should prospect for more gold. You take this as a joke.
D You sell the nugget and think no more about it.

6. YOU LEARN FROM A CONFIDENTIAL SOURCE THAT A POWERFUL CORPORATION IS ABOUT TO GET PERMISSION TO START MINING NEAR YOUR HOME. WOULD YOU:

A Alert the local newspaper and radio station. Form a protest group. Spend all your energy trying to stop your neighborhood from being destroyed.
B Wait for someone else to launch a protest group, join it and help out.

C Don't think that protest will do much good. You sign a petition and give a few dollars to the cause.

D You sell your house to the mining company and clear out.

7. **YOU ARE OFFERED A REALLY GREAT JOB. THE ONLY SNAG IS THAT YOU WOULD HAVE TO LEARN JAPANESE AND PASS AN EXAM AT THE END OF YOUR FIRST SIX MONTHS. IF YOU FAIL THE TEST YOU LOSE THE JOB. WOULD YOU:**

A Take the job and work like crazy to learn Japanese. OK, so it's supposed to be one of the world's hardest languages but so what? If other people have managed it so can you.

B You agonize over whether you could learn such a hard language. You take the job but make contingency plans in case things don't work out.

C You spend ages trying to talk yourself into taking the job but you really don't have what it takes. Eventually the offer is withdrawn.

D You wouldn't even consider taking a job like that. Japanese? They have to be kidding. You even flunked Spanish at school.

8. **YOUR PARTNER CATCHES A SERIOUS ILLNESS. THERE IS HOPE OF A CURE BUT THE TREATMENT IS ONLY AVAILABLE IN SWITZERLAND AND WILL COST MANY THOUSANDS OF DOLLARS. WOULD YOU:**

A Launch a fund and go around soliciting contributions. You devote all your time and energy to this and succeed in raising the funds.

B Try to borrow the money from the bank. You get turned down. You try to raise it from other sources but you don't have what it takes to persuade people to part with their money.

C You are completely overcome by the idea of raising such a huge amount of money. You don't even know where to start.

D You have been defeated from the beginning. The whole idea is just more than you can get your head round.

9. THERE ARE REPORTS OF A MASSIVE FAMINE IN NORTH AFRICA. YOU ARE A DOCTOR AND YOUR CAREER IS GOING VERY WELL. HOWEVER, IN YOUR YOUNGER YEARS YOU WORKED IN A FAMINE-STRICKEN AREA. DO YOU:

A Put your life and career on hold while you volunteer your services.
B Arrange to take some vacation that is owed to you. You won't be able to do very much but you figure that every little bit helps.
C You can't possibly go yourself but you work to raise relief funds.
D You send a contribution to the famine relief fund. Go yourself? No way!

10. YOU DISCOVER THAT YOU ARE SUFFERING FROM AN INCURABLE FORM OF CANCER. YOU ARE NOT FEELING VERY ILL AT THE MOMENT BUT YOUR TIME IS RUNNING OUT. DO YOU:

A Start to campaign to raise funds for medical research. You run sponsored marathons and make public appearances trying to raise awareness about this disease. You are an inspiration to others.
B Try to keep fit, adopt a healthy lifestyle, and investigate alternative therapies.
C Spend the time that remains quietly with your family.
D Roll over and die. What's the point?

ANSWERS

Score 4 points for an A, 3 for a B, 2 for a C, and 1 for a D

35–40 You're a human dynamo! Is there nothing you can't do? You're the sort of person who really makes a difference in this world. However, you tend to get obsessed by a task to the exclusion of everything and everyone else. No one has unlimited energy and, if you use it all for one cause, you won't have much left over for other things. This can make relationships difficult and it will take a very understanding sort of partner to put up with your endless crusades.

25–34 You are very energetic and capable but you also recognize your limitations. You will work very hard at a task dear to your heart but are not totally obsessive about things. You keep a bit of yourself in reserve and therefore your relationships will not suffer as a result of the projects you get involved in. Your lack of total commitment means that you will achieve all that you could but you feel that you need to preserve some balance in your life and this is certainly a wise decision.

15–24 You give up too easily. You know what you want to achieve but you just don't have enough push to get the job done. Your life is a succession of good intentions that didn't work out. This is a shame because you have a good heart and could do so much but you don't have enough staying power to get the job done when things get rough. With just a bit more effort you could really make a difference.

Under 15 What a waste of space you are! You are one of those people who are licked even before they start. If you won't put anything in to life what do you expect to get out of it? No one looks to you for anything because they can see that you have nothing to give. You'd better try stiffening your backbone or you'll find that life just passes you by.

What would you sacrifice for your beliefs?

The world we live in can be very intolerant of different beliefs and ideals. Many people try to force their opinons on others and some will use extreme measures to acheive this. Therefore, standing up for your own beliefs can be uncomfortable, if not dangerous. But if you don't want others to walk all over you there comes a point where you have to make a stand. The question is, how willing are you to suffer for your beliefs? Would you put up with bullying, persecution, or even death? Or would you cave in and sacrifice your beliefs in return for a comfortable existence? That's what this quiz aims to find out.

1

A worker joins your company. He is unpopular with other people because of his ethnic origin. Would you:

A Make a point of befriending him even though it would make you unpopular.
B Try to convince your co-workers that his ethnic background doesn't matter but they refuse to listen to you. You decide it is better to say nothing.
C Adopt the attitude of the majority even though you know inside that it is wrong.

2

You have a strong commitment to a political party. Would you:

A Talk about your views constantly to your family and friends and try to persuade them to share them even though you are aware that this is very irritating.
B Air your views occasionally but only in a way that does not annoy people.
C Keep your views to yourself while feeling guilty that you are not more politically active.

3

Would you have faced the Spanish Inquisition?

A Yes, you have to confront evil at whatever cost.
B No, though I would have hated what they did I wouldn't be brave enough to confront them.
C Are you crazy? I'd keep as far away from them as possible.

4

Do you feel that you have particularly strong principles?

A Yes, there are many subjects about which I feel very strongly.
B Yes, but I don't like having to defend my views to other people.
C No, I don't usually believe in anything very strongly.

5

You are invited to dinner by your boy/girlfriend's parents. They serve something that you cannot eat for religious reasons. Would you:

A Explain that eating this particular food is against your principles. You hope that by being open you will avoid future problems.

B Pretend to pick at the food but when asked if everything is OK immediately say you're ill and apologize for not being able to eat your dinner.

C Eat the meal and say nothing. It's not worth making a fuss.

6

You go to a public meeting where some local issue is being debated. You find that your views are not in tune with the vast majority of your neighbors. Do you:

A Stand up and try to persuade everyone to your view even though this will make you unpopular.

B Express the opposing view by pretending to play devil's advocate.

C Keep quiet. You have to live next to these people so why upset them?

7

You discover that the company you work for is employing child labor in the Far East. If you blow the whistle both you and your co-workers will lose your jobs. Do you:

A Go straight to the newspapers. You couldn't live with yourself if you let this practice continue.

B You go to your boss and tell him what you know. You ask him to use his influence to get the practice changed.

C You write anonymously to the company telling them you know what they are up to.

8

Your boss has very strong opinions with which you disagree. He insists in discussing them at every opportunity. Do you:

A Argue with him and hope that your honesty and outspokenness will count in your favor.

B Take a very cautious line in which you try to ask questions rather than contradict his arguments.

C Appear to agree enthusiastically with all he says. You know a road to promotion when you see one.

9

There's an election coming and everyone in your cul-de-sac has put up posters supporting the same candidate except for you who supports a rival. Would you:

A Put up a poster for your own candidate even though it may have a negative effect on relations with your neighbors.

B Don't put up any poster. It wouldn't do any good and it might cause friction with people you like.

C Put up a poster for the same candidate as everyone else. It's only a poster for goodness' sake!

10

You see a gang of teenagers abusing an elderly man. Do you:

A Dive straight in and give 'em hell. There is no way you will put up with this type of bullying.

B You try to talk politely to the kids and persuade them to leave the old man alone.

C You walk on by. Who knows which of them has a knife?

ANSWERS

Mostly As

Are you the martyr! No one can fault you on the strength of your character but you do seem determined to put people's backs up wherever you go. Is this because you really care about truth and justice or is it something to do with needing attention? You would probably get better results if you didn't charge straight at everyone who opposes you. You seem in many ways to be as doctrinaire as they are. Maybe you should try a softer, more persuasive line sometimes.

Mostly Bs

Your heart is in the right place but you have some problems in the courage department. You are very good at trying to be reasonable but you are aware that sometimes people simply won't listen to reason and, when this happens, you need to resort to stronger tactics. This is where you fall down because, when push comes to shove, you are just not that brave. But let's face it, the vast majority of the human race suffers from the same problem so you are not exactly unusual.

Mostly Cs

How do you look at yourself in the mirror? You have elastic principles and no courage at all. You would let anyone do anything just so long as they let you alone. You think that you are playing it safe but you don't realize that if enough people thought the way you do the whole world would soon be ruled by tyrants. Why don't you get up and fight for a cause you believe in while you still have the chance?

How much would you endure for love?

Love is supposed to be the most important thing in the world. We all tell ourselves that it counts for more than anything else. The world is full of songs, books, films, poems, and greeting cards that all extol love as the most important thing in life. But is it true? When you seriously think about it, how much would you go through for love? Fortunately for most of us we never get tested in any extreme way. But if you watch TV or read the newspapers you can't avoid stories of those whose relationship is tested to the max and this causes us to wonder whether we could survive such situations. Here is a chance to consider just how strong your heart really is.

1. **YOU LOSE YOUR JOB AND YOUR HOME. YOU END UP LIVING IN A CHEAP MOTEL AND SURVIVING ON HANDOUTS. HOW WOULD YOU AND YOUR PARTNER COPE?**

A We'd be just fine. If anything the problems would bring us closer together.

B I can't pretend this would be easy. We'd suffer a lot but I think our love would survive as long as the problem didn't continue for too long.

C We probably wouldn't last more than a couple of weeks. We both need a comfortable lifestyle to be happy.

2. **YOUR CHILD HAS STRAYED INTO THE ROAD AND IS IN THE PATH OF AN ONCOMING CAR. WOULD YOU THROW YOURSELF INTO ITS PATH AND ATTEMPT A RESCUE?**

A Yes, I would react instinctively.

B I'd like to think I would but the truth is that I often hesitate in moments of crisis. I'm afraid I might wait a split second too long.

C My sense of self-preservation is too strong. However much I wanted to do it I think I'd freeze before throwing myself in front of the car.

3. **YOUR PARTNER LEAVES YOU FOR SOMEONE ELSE. WOULD YOU:**

A Remain devoted. Hope constantly that you will get back together.

B Try for a reconciliation but when it doesn't work, accept the situation and move on.

C Abandon this failed relationship and move on.

4. **YOU AND YOUR PARTNER ARE SEPARATED BY CIRCUMSTANCES BEYOND YOUR CONTROL. YOU HAVE NO WAY OF KNOWING IF OR WHEN YOU WILL BE REUNITED. WOULD YOU:**

A Stay completely faithful even if you had to wait for many years.

B Wait a few years but eventually give up and start a new life with someone else.

C You don't see any point in waiting—life's too short. You look out for a new partner right away.

5. **YOUR PARTNER IS SUFFERING FROM A LONG AND DEBILITATING ILLNESS. DO YOU:**

A Provide constant care and encouragement even though life has become very hard for you.

B You try to cope but after a few years it becomes too much and you leave.

C You leave straight away. You didn't sign up as a nurse.

6. **YOU MEET SOMEONE ELSE AND BECOME QUITE OBSESSED WITH THEM. WHAT HAPPENS?**

A You make a heroic effort to get over your obsession. You could never bear to cause your partner pain.

B You have an affair but then return to your partner and ask to be forgiven.

C You go off with your new love. You tell yourself, "We have no control over who we love."

7. **YOU AND YOUR PARTNER SPLIT AND BEGIN A TUG-OF-LOVE OVER THE KIDS. WHAT HAPPENS?**

A You can't possibly live without your children. You fight for your life to gain custody.

B You decide that it would be better for the children to stay with your partner, even though that decision breaks your heart.

C You give up seeing the kids as it's just too hard. It's time for a new start.

8. WAR BREAKS OUT. YOUR PARTNER ENDS UP BEHIND ENEMY LINES. WOULD YOU ATTEMPT A RESCUE?

A Yes, there's no way I could go on living without my partner. I'd risk anything.

B Truthfully? Probably not. I'd want to but I'm not hero material.

C No, there's no point in getting killed in some foolish mission.

9. YOU GET OFFERED A REALLY EXCELLENT JOB IN ANOTHER COUNTRY. YOUR PARTNER ISN'T WILLING TO RELOCATE. WHAT DO YOU DO?

A No job would ever tempt me to leave my partner. I'd turn the offer down.

B This is a tough one. I think I'd be angry with my partner for being so unreasonable. If persuasion failed I'd probably end up going on my own.

C I'm ambitious and wouldn't let a relationship get in my way. Successful people can always find partners.

10. YOUR PARTNER NEEDS A KIDNEY TRANSPLANT AND MIRACULOUSLY YOU ARE A PERFECT MATCH. WOULD YOU AGREE TO BE A DONOR?

A Yes, without hesitation.

B This is a major decision but I think that in the end I could overcome my fears and go ahead with the operation.

C No way! All my organs are staying right where they are thank you.

ANSWERS

Mostly As

If your replies are all heart-felt then you are an extraordinarily devoted person. You would suffer just about anything life could throw at you for the sake of those you love. Some people would doubt whether you could really live up to the very high standards you have set yourself but it is beyond doubt that there are such extraordinary individuals in the world and it may be that you are one of them.

Mostly Bs

You are quite realistic about your reactions. You know that, though you want very much to give love, sometimes you are simply not strong enough to do everything that might be asked of you. It is very sensible to know your limitations because it prevents you or those around you having false expectations. The situations outlined above are actually quite extreme, most likely, in real life you will actually be able to solve most of the problems that come your way.

Mostly Cs

You are clearly quite selfish and unwilling to invest much in a relationship. You regard people as being disposable and easily replaced. This attitude won't bring you much long term happiness because the only people who will put up with you will be of a similar turn of mind. This doesn't look like the making of a good partnership.

Would you really want to be irresistible?

Being attractive to the opposite sex, is for many people, a major aim in life. There is a multi-billion dollar industry built on the desire of people to look better, dress better, smell better, and all so that they can attract a better class of partner. Being irresistible to members of the opposite sex is a common enough fantasy but would it actually be as much fun as you think? This test invites you to explore the idea and see whether being irresistible would really turn you on.

1. **A spray is discovered that, when applied discreetly, attracts members of the opposite sex like bees to nectar. It is, however, very expensive. What would you do?**
   A I'm not rich but I'd find a way to get the money even if I had to rob a bank. This is just too good to pass up.
   B Yes, I would give it a try though, at that price, I doubt whether I'd use it often even if it worked.
   C I bet it wouldn't work. Even if it did the cost would put me off.
   D I'd hate the idea that people were only attracted to me by some chemical trick. I wouldn't use it.

2. **You unexpectedly become a star and are ruthlessly pursued by people who want to get to know you much better. Do you:**
   A Enjoy it. This is exactly the sort of life you always dreamt of.
   B Enjoy it sometimes but occasionally go out incognito so you can enjoy a little privacy.

C You find it hard to cope with. You go out less because you hate being pestered.

D You hate that people are attracted only to your looks. You go into hiding and leave the celebrity lifestyle behind.

3. **Would you have plastic surgery to enhance your sex appeal?**

A Yes, of course. There is always room for improvement.

B Yes, but nothing too drastic.

C Only to remove an obvious blemish. Otherwise I wouldn't bother.

D I wouldn't dream of it. I would want people to like me just as I am.

4. **You are so sexy that you attract the attentions of a stalker. Would you:**

A Feel flattered. OK, it's a little scary but it's also quite exciting.

B You're terrified and call the cops. Even so you see it as a confirmation of just how gorgeous you are.

C You are really spooked and begin to wonder whether you shouldn't do something to attract less attention.

D The whole episode disgusts you. How can anyone get so obsessed on the basis of someone else's appearance?

5. **Whenever you go out members of the opposite sex pester you. Would you:**

A Really enjoy the attention. Collect phone numbers. Have fun.

B Enjoy the attention most of the time but wish occasionally for a night off.

C Find it all a bit oppressive. You feel you can't move without people watching you.

D You are furious that people can behave in such a stupid and shallow manner.

6. **Your partner becomes jealous and possessive because of all the attention you get. Would you:**

A Tell them if they can't cope with it they can leave. This is what your life is like.

B Tell them that all the adulation means nothing. It has nothing to do with your relationship.

C You agree that it's a nuisance and you make great efforts to avoid the attention.

D You agree that this is destroying your relationship. You decide to move away and start a new sort of life with your partner.

7. **You find yourself in trouble with the jealous partner of someone who has become obsessed with you. Do you:**

A Say that it's hardly your fault if people are attracted to you.

B Apologize but point out that there isn't a lot you can do about it. You've done nothing to encourage this person.

C Feel upset that you are the cause of such unhappiness even though it's not your fault. You try to explain to your obsessed fan that this must stop.

D Tell them both to keep away from you in future or you will involve the law.

8. **You are advised to insure your good looks for a huge sum. Would you?**

A Yes, with these looks I would be crazy not to.

B Yes, it might seem vain but it makes sense when you think about it.

C No, you can't see yourself spending money on something like that.

D No, you think such behavior is stupid.

9. **Someone who despairs of ever attracting your attention commits suicide. Some people think you are to blame. Do you:**

A Shrug it off. Lots of people are obsessed with you. What's new?

B You feel sorry but don't really see what you could have done.

C You are very upset. You feel that in some obscure way you are responsible.

D You are devastated that something as superficial as your looks could have precipitated a tragedy.

10. **As you age your charms start to fade. Would you:**

A Fight the signs of aging with every weapon at your disposal.

B Fight until the signs are unmistakable then give up. You don't want to look stupid.

C Do only sensible things like taking exercise and eating healthily. You aren't interested in artificial aids.

D Accept ageing as natural. You don't think it is important to fight against it.

ANSWERS

Score 4 points for an A, 3 for a B, 2 for a C, and 1 for a D

35–40 You are simply made for the life of a sex symbol. In fact you're so single-minded about it that you're not really fit for much else. You are only happy when enjoying the admiration and desire of others. This isn't a very mature view of life but there is not much you can do about it. Deprived of this sort of attention you would wither and fade like a flower deprived of water. While you remain young and desirable you will be able to indulge your taste for adulation as much as you like but eventually time will catch up with you and then you will have serious problems trying to adapt to a life where people no longer find you so alluring.

25–34 You are keen to be loved and admired but you have a slightly queasy feeling that your lifestyle is not all it's cracked up to be. You are torn between a strong need to be attractive to other people and a sneaky feeling that your behavior is shallow and won't bring you any long-term happiness. You have just enough self-knowledge to realize that everything in your life is not so great but you seem to lack the ability to change. You drift along enjoying your popularity but are always aware that the clock is ticking.

15–24 You really don't buy into all this sex symbol nonsense. You don't like the fact that people are only interested in you as a sex object and you feel, quite rightly, that your personality and character should count for something. Why can't people see beyond your looks to the person inside? You would love to have a proper relationship with someone who didn't care too much about physical attraction.

Under 15 Being irresistible is just not your thing at all. You do your best to avoid attracting people simply in physical terms. It's tough because, however hard you try people are always attracted to you. However, you are really quite serious-minded and determined to live a life that is meaningful and fulfilling. You are determined to be taken seriously as a person and to show people that there is far more to you than just a sexy smile.

HOW VISUAL ARE YOU?

This octagon has an octagonal hole in the center of it. What you have to do is cut up the figure into specific shapes and re-arrange them in such a way that they make a star, also with an octagonal hole in the center. People are firmly divided into those who have a strong visual sense and those who do not. (It is unusual to be slightly visual.) This puzzle is tough enough to sort out those who visualize easily from those who do not. The original puzzle (created by Henry Dudeney in the early twentieth century), gave no hint as to how it might be solved. That seems a trifle harsh so let's just say that by the time you've worked out the answer you'll probably be seeing stars! Turn to page 254 to see the solution.

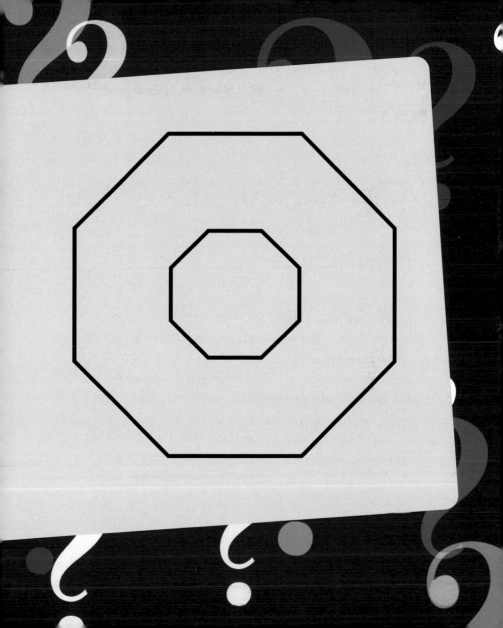

Is there a perfect match for you?

Many people believe that everyone has a perfect partner somewhere. All you have to do is find that person. But would you recognize this person if you ever met them? Have you ever stopped to wonder what your perfect match might be like? Are you mainly influenced by looks, personality, or character? Would your partner need to have a background like your own or are you ready and willing to adapt to someone with a different life experience? Are you bothered by things like qualifications or income? The following test is designed to give you a bit of insight into what sort of person would really make you happy.

1. HOW IMPORTANT IS IT THAT YOUR PARTNER BE GOOD-LOOKING?

A Very important. I couldn't love an ugly person.

B Good looks are certainly something I'd look for but there are other factors.

C I could love someone who was plain if they had the right personality.

D Looks are superficial and fade over time. I go for more important qualities.

2. HOW IMPORTANT IS IT THAT YOU HAVE SHARED INTERESTS?

A Not very important. You share your interests with friends, not your partner.

B It would be nice to have things in common but I'm not holding my breath.

C Some shared interests are essential for a relationship to work.

D I'm looking for a soul mate with whom I can share everything.

3. COULD YOU ONLY MARRY SOMEONE WITH A COMPATIBLE PERSONALITY?

A You could marry anyone. There are plenty of couples who have totally different personalities and they manage to get along.

B I would certainly try to avoid anyone whose personality was too different from mine.

C I think personality is very important. I'd want us to be very alike in many ways.

D Personality is vital. I could never love anyone who wasn't in harmony with me.

4. WOULD YOU CONSIDER A PARTNER WHO CAME FROM A DIFFERENT SOCIAL BACKGROUND?

A I'd never let a thing like that get in the way of my love.

B That sort of thing shouldn't make any difference, though I accept it often does. I think we should follow our hearts.

C It can work but there are always a lot of problems. I'd give it a try if I really loved the person.

D It's not that I'm snobbish but it would just be too difficult.

5. DO YOU BELIEVE THAT THERE IS ONE PERFECT PERSON FOR YOU?

A No. I think you can be happy with just about anyone if the conditions are right.

B I'm sure that there are many people I could be happy with.

C There are only a few people who would make perfect partners. It's very hard to find the right one.

D I do believe that somewhere there is one perfect love for me.

6. SUPPOSE YOU HAD, WHAT YOU THOUGHT, WAS THE PERFECT RELATIONSHIP AND IT BROKE UP?

A I wouldn't be surprised, lots of couples split up. I'd just find someone else.

B I'd work really hard to stop that happening but it still might. I'm sure I'd eventually find someone else.

C A relationship like that should be rock solid. If it failed I'm sure I'd find it very hard to start again.

D I'd be destroyed. I really can't contemplate such a thing happening.

7. ONCE YOU HAD YOUR PERFECT PARTNER WOULD YOU EVER BE TEMPTED TO FOOL AROUND?

A Everyone has the odd affair. It's what stops you getting bored. As long as you don't get caught it's really quite good for a relationship.

B I'd try to be faithful but, if I'm honest, I must admit that I might stray occasionally.

C I don't think I would be unfaithful. I really don't approve of that sort of thing.

D I would never be unfaithful. That would be such a lousy thing to do.

8. WHAT IF YOUR FRIENDS DIDN'T LIKE YOUR PARTNER? WOULD YOU STILL GO AHEAD AND GET HITCHED?

A Absolutely not. My friends are really important to me.

B That would make life hard. I'd try to change my friends' minds but if that didn't work it might be time to say goodbye to my partner.

C Friends come and go. If they aren't supportive about something so important to me maybe it's time to find new friends.

D Our relationship will be so perfect, we won't need *any* friends.

9. **YOUR PARTNER IS NOT TOO CRAZY ABOUT SOME OF YOUR PERSONAL HABITS. HOW FAR WOULD YOU CHANGE TO ACCOMMODATE THESE CRITICISMS?**

A Love me or leave me, that's what I say.

B I'd make a few changes but I'd expect my partner to make some as well.

C I know I'm not perfect and I'd expect to make some changes.

D You can't be that close without making efforts to adapt to each other. I have no objection to changing.

10. **YOU AND YOUR PARTNER HAVE A BIG FIGHT. THINGS ARE SAID THAT CAN NEVER BE TAKEN BACK. WHAT WOULD YOU DO?**

A This sounds like The End to me.

B We will probably get over it this time but it sounds as though there are some hard times ahead.

C Arguments happen in all relationships. You just have to work hard at putting them behind you.

D This relationship is solid. It could survive a direct nuclear strike if necessary.

ANSWERS

Mostly As
Your attitude about love is really quite immature. You are attracted by superficial things and don't have much intention of committing seriously to a relationship. You might have a perfect partner somewhere but it would have to be someone as shallow as you are. To be honest, the two of you are unlikely to have much of a relationship. Let's hope that you are really young and inexperienced and that, as you grow, you will get wiser.

Mostly Bs
You are certainly willing to try for a perfect relationship but may not yet have what it takes. Your responses show you to be well-meaning but a little half-hearted. Relationships require a high level of commitment and sometimes you don't really sound as though you have what it takes. Maybe in time you'll learn to distinguish what is important from what is superficial.

Mostly Cs
Your attitude is very mature. You know just how hard it is to commit to someone and you are prepared to go the distance. You know how important it is to look beyond the obvious and concentrate on more important matters. If there is a perfect partner waiting for you then that is one very lucky person. You are the romantic equivalent of a solid gold ingot.

Mostly Ds
Have you ever considered that you are little too intense? You have romantic notions that border on the obsessive. No one will ever be able to live up to your expectations. It sounds from your responses that you want to be one half of Siamese twins. A relationship like that would be hell for both partners. To be happy people need a little space and independence. Why not relax a little and try for a relationship that has room for both individuals to breathe occasionally?

Would you really want to date a star?

We live in a celebrity culture. Just about everyone wants to be rich and famous or, if that is not an option for ourselves, the next best thing is to be associated with people who are rich and famous. The attractions are obvious, but what about the down side? If you were able to date a star would you really be able to cope? Would your story have a happy ending like *Notting Hill* (where a famous actress played by Julia Roberts is wooed and won by Hugh Grant who plays the owner of a small bookshop)? Or is it more likely that the whole thing would turn into a nightmare? Try our quiz to find out.

1. YOUR STAR MAKES $5M PER MOVIE. YOU WON'T MAKE THAT KIND OF MONEY IN A LIFETIME. WHAT HAPPENS?

A Money makes no difference to our very special relationship.
B We always "go Dutch." We make a great effort not to let the difference in income bother us.
C We find the situation a bit awkward but do our best to ignore the problems.
D We have constant quarrels about money. It puts the whole relationship under a strain.

2. WHENEVER YOU ARE OUT ON A DATE YOU GET BOTHERED BY AUTOGRAPH HUNTERS. WHAT HAPPENS?

A You love the whole celebrity lifestyle. You are flattered to be with someone who is so in demand.
B It's a bit of a drag but you appreciate that it comes with the territory.
C You resent the interruptions and encourage your friend to go out incognito.
D The fans drive you mad but your friend is adamant that being nice to them is part of the job. It causes constant friction between you.

3. THE PAPARAZZI GET PICTURES OF YOU BOTH ON A BEACH WITH ALMOST NO CLOTHES ON. WHAT HAPPENS?

A You feel quite proud. You both look good and the pics appear in all the best celebrity magazines.
B You take it philosophically. You realize that this sort of thing is part of dating a star.
C You feel deeply embarrassed. This intrusion violated an intimate moment.
D You're furious and decide to punch the next press photographer you see.

4. JOURNALISTS MAKE FUN OF THE FACT THAT YOU HAVE A RATHER UNGLAMOROUS JOB. WHAT HAPPENS:

A Ignore it utterly. You are very secure and know your own worth as a person.
B You feel a bit hurt but you know that your friend is quite happy with you as you are.
C Your friend doesn't seem bothered but you wonder privately whether these attacks will have a bad effect on your relationship.
D Your friend tries to encourage you to improve your position in life. You are afraid that if you can't do it then the relationship is doomed.

5. YOUR FRIEND LANDS A PART IN A BIG MOVIE BUT MUST GO AWAY ON LOCATION FOR SEVERAL MONTHS. WHAT HAPPENS?

A You are delighted that your friend's career is going so well. You hope to be able to visit and watch part of the film being made.
B You are pleased for your friend but worry that your relationship won't survive the separation.
C You feel insecure. You've heard about the sort of things that happen on location.
D You are insanely jealous and try to persuade your friend not to go.

6. YOU GO TO THE PREMIERE OF YOUR FRIEND'S MOVIE BUT FIND THAT YOU ARE LARGELY IGNORED BY EVERYONE. WHAT HAPPENS?

A You realize that this is not about you. You are pleased that your friend has done so well and spend a pleasant evening rubbing shoulders with the stars.

B You feel a bit left out but still manage to enjoy the evening.

C You feel hurt and angry even though you know that this is unreasonable behavior.

D You see now that you could never fit into your friend's life. You realize that the relationship is over.

7. YOU AND YOUR FRIEND DECIDE TO MARRY BUT YOU ARE ASKED TO SIGN A PRENUPTIAL AGREEMENT THAT LIMITS YOUR RIGHTS IN THE EVENT OF A DIVORCE. WHAT HAPPENS?

A You sign the agreement without any questions. You had expected it anyway.

B You sign but only after your lawyers have negotiated the best deal they can for you.

C You sign it but feel hurt that the person you love seems to need this sort of safety net.

D You choose not to sign the agreement even if your decision means that the wedding is off.

8. YOUR FRIEND'S NAME IS ROMANTICALLY LINKED BY THE PRESS TO ANOTHER STAR. WHAT HAPPENS?

A You laugh it off. The papers are always making this sort of stuff up.

B You think that it's untrue but start to experience feelings of insecurity.

C You pay a private investigator to discover the truth.

D You fly into a jealous rage and accuse your friend of having betrayed you.

9. YOUR FRIEND'S CAREER TAKES A DIVE AND SUDDENLY THE PARTY IS OVER. WHAT HAPPENS?

A You lose interest. It was the celebrity lifestyle that really attracted you.

B You try to carry on as if nothing has changed but feel secretly disappointed.

C You find that this sudden change takes a lot of the pressure off the relationship and you get on better than ever.

D You are delighted that your friend has, at last, been brought down to earth. You now try hard to build a "normal" relationship.

10. THE RELATIONSHIP ENDS BADLY. YOUR LAWYER URGES YOU TO LAUNCH A PALIMONY SUIT.

A You agree. You deserve compensation for all the support you have given.

B You agree reluctantly and are happy to settle out of court.

C You don't agree. You wouldn't want to endure all the pressure of a court case.

D You don't agree. You have always despised the celebrity lifestyle and never wanted the money anyway.

ANSWERS

An A scores 4 points, a B scores 3, a C scores 2 and a D scores 1

35–40 You have bought into the celebrity myth big time. You are perfect for this sort of life and will almost certainly succeed in it. Given the sort of help and contacts that your friend can offer you will probably end up being a star in your own right. The celebrity world may be shallow, materialist, and ephemeral but it is clearly your true spiritual home. You ask nothing more out of life than this.

25–34 You enjoy the celebrity lifestyle but are possibly not strong enough to make it work for you. The trouble is that you can never really escape from your origins. You always feel as though you are out of place in the celebrity world and that people think you are a fake. You struggle hard to make the relationship work but at best your chances of success are no better than 50/50.

15–24 You are clearly in the wrong relationship. However much you like and admire this person you will never be able to fit into the celebrity life. You are far too tied to your own system of values and you will always feel that your friend's friends are shallow, materialistic, and false. There are just too many negatives for you to cope with here. The only way out would be to bring the relationship to a gentle end. That way you could both look back on it without bitterness.

Under 15 This relationship has been doomed from day one. Whatever feelings you have for each other are simply not strong enough to survive all the pressures that celebrities live with. You clearly dislike everything about the world of the rich and famous but there is no way that your friend would ever give it all up to be with you. Your only hope of getting out of this without suffering emotional damage is to regard the whole thing as a quick fling—a few weeks of fun and then a quick goodbye.

Are you ready for world domination?

There used to be a song, *If I ruled the world*. But what if you did? Could you handle it? What would you do? Would you use your power for the good of mankind or do you think that that much power would corrupt you? This is your chance to think the whole issue through. The test will establish not only whether you are ready for absolute power, but what sort of leader you would be—a benign dictator or a ruthless tyrant. At least this way, if the day ever comes, you'll know exactly what to expect.

1

Are you the sort of person who always knows how everybody else is messing up?

A Of course! Why are people so dumb?
B I often see people acting unwisely.
C I don't like to interfere but occasionally you see a situation where you have no choice.
D I try not to be judgmental. You don't always know all the circumstances.

2

Do you always offer people your advice whether or not they've asked for it?

A People have often commented on how good I am at giving advice.
B I try to wait until I am asked but sometimes advice slips out before I can help myself.
C I make it a rule not to offer advice unless people really want it.
D The only time I offer advice is if I'm being paid for it.

3

Can you remember the last time you made a mistake?

A Um, it was a Tuesday afternoon. 1998 perhaps? Maybe 1997.
B I don't make that many mistakes and when I do I patch them up quickly.
C I'm only human. I make mistakes all the time but I try to learn from them.
D I'm constantly racked with guilt about all the things I get wrong.

4

Are you a control freak?

A I don't like that expression. I just happen to be good at supervising others.
B Sometimes I find it hard not to take control. I find that others can be so unreliable.
C I'm not big on control. Most people do better if you use a very light touch.
D I would never try to control people. I like to lead by example.

5

Do you feel that you have God on your side?

A Just try getting in my way. You'll soon find out.
B I like to think that I'm on the side of the angels.
C I always hope I'm doing the right thing but who knows for sure?
D I wouldn't presume to say anything like that.

6

Would you like to make the world a better place?

A I already do, but if I had more power I could do a much better job.
B Yes, I'd certainly like to try and I think I have a lot to offer.
C We all feel that way but it isn't an easy thing to do.
D I don't honestly think I have the ability however much I might want to.

7

Is there any limit to your ambitions?

A How high is the sky?
B I believe that I could achieve great things in the right circumstances.
C I have ambitions but I try to stay realistic.
D I'm not really that ambitious. I just want things like a good job, a nice house, and a loving family.

8

How do you feel about people who disagree with you?

A They're creeps who are up to no good. They need to be controlled.
B I suspect their motives and methods. I use all my ability to oppose them.
C They are entitled to their view, I will always listen to constructive criticism.
D People have every right to criticize. I am aware that I am a long way from perfect.

9

Do you have a thick skin?

A We're talking alligator hide with a coat of Teflon.
B I don't let things get to me too much.
C Criticism always hurts but I manage to put it behind me.
D I'm probably oversensitive but I find criticism deeply hurtful.

10

Would people be happier if they all did what you told them?

A How could you doubt?
B I'm sure I could make a better job of things than the people who are in charge now.
C I'd do my best to make people happier but it wouldn't be easy.
D I'm not at all sure that one person can make that much difference. Certainly I don't think I could.

ANSWERS

Give yourself 4 points for an A, 3 for a B, 2, for a C and 1 for a D

35–40 Your desire for personal power is outstripped only by your self-confidence. You are the sort of person who starts revolutions. You think that you're working for the general good and that people ought to be grateful and you just can't understand why some seem to doubt your motives and ability. You don't take kindly to criticism or to any sort of interference in your plans. If you are as able and determined as you think you may well end up running a major corporation or even the whole country. On the other hand, if you are just a bag of hot air you'll probably end up driving a cab.

25–34 You have a lot of confidence in your ability but it is tempered by a little realism. Even so you tend to overestimate yourself. You need to keep your feet much more firmly on the ground. If you do that then you might actually become a valuable person who can make great contributions as a leader. But if you let your confidence become overblown you will end up as just another megalomaniac and, to be honest, the world has enough of those already.

15–24 There is no way that you are ever going to rule the world but you know that and you are quite happy with the situation. Your abilities and ambitions are very happily balanced. You will be able to achieve all sorts of good things in life without being in danger of your ego becoming inflated. Crazy notions of domination just don't tempt you at all. Also you have excellent powers of self-criticism and you are not afraid to hear criticism from others. This is a source of great strength to you.

Under 15 You are lacking in ambition and self-confidence. You might well have some ability but we will never find out because you are too lacking in self-assurance to do anything about it. What you need is a really hefty dose of esteem because, at the moment, you are really selling yourself short. How can other people ever be persuaded to give you opportunities when you seem so self-doubting? Unless you take charge right now, you will lead a life of miserable underachievement and you will have no one to blame but yourself.

PAGE 210: THE BEST ROUTE

If you're really ingenious you will have been able to get your total down to a mere 14 strokes. If you follow our diagram below from A to Z you will see how it's done. We have deliberately not joined up the lines so that you can see the route clearly.

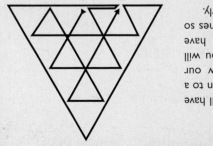

PAGE 234: HOW VISUAL ARE YOU?

As you can see, the solution is really very simple. The odd thing is that the majority of people either see it straight away in their mind's eye, or they never get it at all. Most puzzles yield to a bit of persistence and logic but visual reasoning seems to be one of those knacks that you either have or you don't.

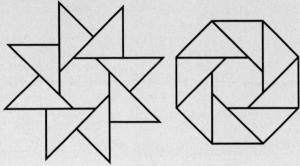

PAGE 96: PULLING THE WOOL OVER YOUR EYES.

It is amazing how hard it is to spot something that's not there. It's like that embarrassing moment when a friend decides to shave off a beard or moustache and you completely fail to notice any difference. In this case the change is a bit more subtle than that. The rhyme has been rewritten avoiding any use of the letter E.

PAGE 116: THE HOLE TRUTH

Poke the tip of your finger through the hole and use it to push the coin. You were asked to "push the coin through the hole" and now you have.

PAGE 150: THE ANSWER IS OBVIOUS!

We told you the answer was obvious and it is. The letters round the two figures can be rearranged to form the word OBVIOUS, with the V missing. Let's hope that you took a quick glance at the puzzle and saw immediately past all the red herrings that were being dragged across your path. If, in spite of our warnings, you came up with clever theories about this puzzle then, sadly, you only have yourself to blame.

PAGE 186: PRACTICAL MAGIC

Crumple the paper and float it on the water. Quickly light a match, set light to the top of the paper, then invert the tumbler over the burning paper. As the flame burns up all the oxygen under the tumbler the water will rush in and leave your coin high and dry.

PUZZLE ANSWERS

PAGE 20: JUST HOW PERSISTANT ARE YOU?

There are actually over 640 possible routes.

PAGE 44: WHAT IS THE LINK?

They are all anagrams of boys' names: Steve, Neil, Daniel, Andrew, Lee, Silas, Eric, Cyril. If you got it in less than ten seconds congratulate yourself on your perspicacity. Anything under a couple of minutes is not bad. If you were still struggling five minutes after you started, then words are clearly not your strong point. Don't worry though, word skills are only a part of intelligence and by no means all of it.

PAGE 78: THE MOVING FINGER WRITES . . .

Draw your circle in the normal way. Then fold a corner of the paper in until the very tip of the corner points to the center of your circle. Now you can run your pencil along the folded portion until it reaches the center where you can make a dot without having the pencil ever having left the paper.